the BELIEF Blueprint

Uncover the Universal Blueprint for Building Belief One Step at a Time

BY SPENCER PETTIT

ACKNOWLEDGEMENTS

This book wouldn't exist without the support and input of many individuals. Each name below represents someone who touched me and shaped this message in a significant way. I can't thank you enough for the time and wisdom you have shared with me.

My wife, Laura Pettit, for your pure heart and unfailing belief in me

My parents and editors, Tom & Janae Pettit, for always supporting me in everything I pursued in life

My wise (cracking) siblings Tommy, Amanda, Jesse, Mirinda, and Carissa for all the debate and opinion that shaped this message and me

Allyse & Patrick Sedivy for challenging me to go further than I ever thought possible

Emily Wright for believing in me and showing me the way to live with purpose

Doug Castor for sparking the idea to put this message in print

Scottsdale Multimedia for their patience and perspective throughout production

Lucas Marc Design for bringing The Belief Blueprint to life

TABLE OF CONTENTS

INTRODUCTION

Do you know someone who seems to have life easier than everyone else? Everything works out for them. They are surrounded by good friends, money flows to them as they seamlessly move from one job to the next in their career, they have adoring spouses and children. From the outside it would appear that these people have some magic secret, some kind of blueprint for success. The truth is that there is a lot more going on behind the scenes than meets the eye. In fact, successful individuals have usually faced more hardship and have overcome more obstacles than their peers. The difference is not luck, but instead a mastery of a natural process that every successful person has put to the test over and over in their lives. How do I know this? I am one of these people.

A conversation I had with my mother in my early teens is still as clear in my mind today as when it happened. We were talking about some of the great things happening for me at the time and she said, "You just have a charmed life." I wasn't sure exactly what that meant, but I liked how it sounded. Who wouldn't want some enchantment cast on them that guaranteed success? During the hard times since then, this idea has served as a helpful boost to my confidence as I continued on in life, expecting things to work out for the best even when they weren't going my way. I've proven time and time again that my mindset is my greatest asset.

For example, clear back in high school (I could go back further, but we'll save that for later), I made the decision to join the choir. I had watched my older brother and sister have positive experiences in their high school choirs, so I naturally expected the same. After a couple of days in the Freshman Chorale, my choir director asked a few of us to stay after school for "voice lessons."

When my turn came up, I went in and sang some scales as instructed. Admittedly, my range wasn't the best back then, but I thought I did a decent job for a 13-year-old with developing vocal chords. After I was done, the teacher looked at me and said, "Have you ever had a doctor look at your vocal cords?" I was confused by the question. I'd expected a little coaching, maybe, but I'd never expected him to ask about my vocal cords. I shrugged and replied that I hadn't.

"I think you probably should," he said. "You sound like you might have nodes."

Now, for those of you who prefer to keep your vocal talents to yourselves, nodes are like little bundles of scar tissue that can form in the voice box, specifically on your vocal cords. The effect can be pretty drastic. Having nodes can destroy a person's ability to sing well. If professional singers get nodes, they typically have to go in for surgery, or even quit altogether.

I was young, but I knew what nodes were. The choir director was basically telling me that I had an awful tone and would never be a great singer. I understood that, but I wasn't about to let him stop me from pursuing something I wanted. I'd always had a raspy tone to my voice, and even been complimented on it. I'd grown up singing with my family and had even had solos in church and small performances. I couldn't think of a reason to stop singing. So, the next day, I showed up to choir. And the next and the next. Stubbornly, I kept pushing forward, working my hardest to improve my voice, my range, and my understanding of music theory (it helped that I also had been playing the piano for years at this point).

By the time I started my junior year, my singing career had changed quite a bit. Instead of having the choir director concerned about me, I was an important member of the school's top choirs. I tried out for and placed as one of the top high school basses in the state of Arizona my junior and senior years. Three friends and I even started a four-member a cappella group that performed for hundreds and even thousands at a time. I most definitely consider myself a singer.

Of course, this isn't a book about me (that book would be much shorter and much less interesting), and it definitely isn't a book about my passion for music. This is a book about confidence. About *your* confidence. This is a book about reaching your goals. This is about pushing forward and achieving all the things you've always dreamed of—and how to harness your brain and self to make that happen.

My goal is to make this book to be like a big mirror. I want to show you *you*. I want you to see yourself in these pages (imperfections and all) and yet realize the potential within yourself to become something amazing—and then I want to show you how to climb for that lofty height. You will have a lot of "aha moments" and personalized insights come to you as you read along. Record these in the blank notes pages at the back of the book. Mark these pages up with your highlighter of choice so you can come back to them again and again as you work toward your goals.

But this book isn't about setting the right kinds of goals. There's plenty of other material about that already out there. This is about achieving goals. This isn't so much about looking for future success as it is about evolving you into the person who will achieve whatever kind of success you want. I'm talking about motivation on one level, but I'm really talking about self-actualization—about becoming the very best you that you could ever become. This isn't a pep talk to pump you up; it's a deep dive to connect you with what already moves you and then help you harness that momentum and take it in new directions beyond all limits.

It's time to help you figure out what makes you—the unique, special individual you are—tick, and then you can move forward to the beat of your own metronome to become the you that you've always dreamed of being. Ready?

OVERVIEW

First off, everyone wants to know the secret, right? Why was I able to push forward and ultimately achieve my goal of becoming a good singer? Well, I can tell you one thing it wasn't. It wasn't "The Secret," at least not as most people understand it. It wasn't some mystical power that brought the Universe to its knees and made it bow to my wishes.

It was brutally hard work. It was dogged pursuit of a goal in the face of a sometimes-impossible uphill climb. But it didn't *feel* that way because I knew that I wasn't going to let anything stand in my way—so I didn't. I overcame the obstacles and achieved my goal. Sorry to disappoint, but there is no trick to that. There's no secret. If you really want to do something, you have to get out there and do whatever's required. There are no shortcuts on the road to becoming your best self.

Society would have you believe that the line from where you are (Point A) to where you want to go (Point B) is straight. It's the Cartesian plane you learned about in geometry when you were a kid. You need two points to make a vector, and the fastest way between two points is a straight line, right? Society would have you believe that the path to achieving your goals looks like this:

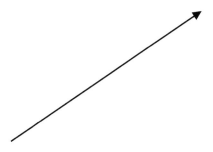

In reality, unlike the controlled world of simple mathematics, things are never quite so clean. I love math; I always have. Math is easy. You have your inputs, they go through defined, measurable processes and you get your outputs. There's no guessing, no grey area. Unfortunately, that's nothing like life. Life is a mess more often than not. Life is a practice in controlled chaos—if you're lucky. The rest of us just suffer from illusions of control.

The fact of the matter is that the path to becoming all you can be looks very different from the straight-line image I just showed you. The reality looks much more like this:

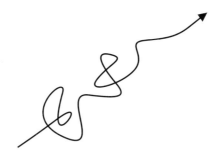

Look a little more true to life? It should. You know the feeling of moving forward and then getting pulled into a completely different direction? You might even feel at times like you're going backwards! How can you possibly navigate that kind of a path when it doesn't seem to make any sense? Well, that is the million-dollar question. This seemingly chaotic path throws most people off their goals just like a bucking bronco. But as you learn the process explained in this book, you will see that you're likely already on the path to personal and financial success. So let's get started by making sense of your brain. We'll talk psychology later, but we're going to talk biology for now.

Three Brains

I am not a doctor and I don't even play one on TV. We're about to dive into a subject that can be far more complicated than most people ever need to understand, myself included. I learned a long time ago not to pretend that I know more than I really do, but thanks to some great mentors and the high availability of complex information out there, I've been able to condense some helpful insights about the human brain and how it affects our every move.

For example, did you know you have three brains? You do. Well, sort of. There's only one big bundle of neurons between your ears, but thanks to the wonders of creation or evolution or whatever you believe in, your brain has roughly three different levels of sophistication—resulting in more brain power than any other creature on this planet.

That large outer level is that of your conscious thought and logic. That's called your cerebral cortex and it contains your "new brain" or neocortex. No other animal (or plant) on earth has a neocortex as complex as what we have here—it's what makes humans human. This is the part of your brain that enables you to plan ahead for what you're going to cook for dinner and then think ahead to make sure you have all the ingredients at home. This is the part of the brain that enables you to make a logical argument and then come up with supporting details. This also happens to be the part of the brain responsible for language.

The next level down in our simple model is the midbrain, which is our center of consciousness. This is the part of your brain responsible for eating, sleeping, vision, hearing, and motor control—everything that lets you know you're alive! This tightly connected experiential pathway to the neocortex is something we share with mammals like wolves, killer whales, chimpanzees, and mice and explains their amazing ability to solve problems. They can run into a difficult situation and think their way out using new basic observations and a developed neocortex. This awareness is what leads some animals, like chimps and otters, to invent rudimentary tools. They don't have a complex neocortex, so their tool creation abilities are limited, but they have the ability to use their surroundings in inventive ways—like putting a stick into a termite mound and then eating all the termites that climb onto the stick.

The final level is the lowest, deepest part of your brain. This is the limbic brain. The limbic brain is also sometimes called your reptilian brain, but I like to call it your "lizard brain." All vertebrates have a limbic brain; it operates instinct. Its job is to keep you alive. Your limbic brain also happens to be responsible for decision-making processes in addition to your survival instincts. It is where we store our memories and, therefore, our feelings. This is the actual location of the "human heart." The autonomic nervous system lives here and controls the balance between fight-or-flight and rest-and-digest responses. Basically, the limbic brain runs your body in order to free your mind (the neocortex and midbrain) to focus on everything else. But that's also a problem, you see: *we can't control the limbic brain.*

This creates an interesting dichotomy in people. Because we live in the neocortex and midbrain, we have this illusion of control over ourselves. Our higher levels of thought and speech are under our control, but our deeper existence and survival instincts are too deep for us to reach directly. What's even worse, the limbic system is extremely powerful. If you've trained enough, you might be able to influence your heart rate with your neocortex, but the limbic brain will prevent you from, say, stopping your heart with a thought—or even slowing your heart to unsafe levels. Thankfully, this doesn't mean there's no hope of being able to understand and control your brain.

You can think of this in terms of a lion tamer at the circus. The trainer really only has an illusion of control. If that lion really wanted to, it could eat the trainer at any time. The trainer couldn't fend off the lion; the lion is too big and too strong. If the lion wanted to get up and leave, the trainer couldn't stop it. However, there's another key principle here. The lion and the trainer have developed a relationship wherein the lion trusts the trainer. If the trainer were to somehow violate that trust and confuse or threaten the lion, bad things would happen (as we've seen in some high profile big cat shows), but the lion will let the trainer run the show under normal circumstances.

Your limbic brain is much the same as that lion. It is totally content to operate in the background and just keep you alive and healthy. It takes input from the neocortex when it makes decisions too, but the decisions still belong to the limbic brain. That's why you can think through all the logical reasons to do something (or not do something) and yet find yourself rebelling against your decision and doing the opposite. If you get out of sync with your limbic brain, this inner voice can sometimes be like a roaring lion. The good news is that, again, just like with the lion, your limbic brain can be trained to apply all its power and authority toward achieving the things you've dreamt up in your neocortex. Now, let's talk about how to sync up with the on inside you.

What, Why, How

Now that you have a basic understanding of how your brain works, you're ready to learn how to make your whole brain work *for* you. In order to understand how to train your brain, you need to first understand how the three levels of the brain relate back to the process of setting and achieving goals and dreams. In that regard, there are three different components to anything you could ever want to do. First, and most obvious, is the "What," next is the "Why," and connecting the two is the "How."

What

This is commonly considered to be the most important part of any goal. What, exactly, do you want to accomplish? If you don't have a What, you'll be much like Alice when she was lost in Wonderland. An excerpt from Lewis Carroll's masterpiece follows:

"Would you tell me, please, which way I ought to go from here?"

"That depends a good deal on where you want to get to," said the Cat.

"I don't much care where–" said Alice.

"Then it doesn't matter which way you go," said the Cat.

"–so long as I get somewhere," Alice added as an explanation.

"Oh, you're sure to do that," said the Cat, "if you only walk long enough."

This little exchange is a beautiful example of how so many people go through life. They don't really know What they want, so they just wander from fad to fad, feeling empty. This emptiness is typically a symptom of setting your sights on fleeting physical possessions as a measure of success. The real measure of success is how much knowledge, or *confidence,* you gained along the way. For example, finally getting the house of your dreams in and of itself is just a one-time exciting experience. However, *knowing* that you can get the house of your dreams again and again, now that is powerful. Do you see the difference?

Knowing your What is critically important, but it will only have lasting effects if it changes you for the better. You've probably heard about lottery winners or pro athletes who suddenly come into a lot of money and lose most of it a short time later. They may have had a goal to have lots of money, but their What was not to be wealthy for the rest of their lives. Though they may appear similar, these two goals couldn't be more different! Setting the right What in your sights will ensure lasting satisfaction, instead of quick gratification followed by more emptiness. What you really want is confidence.

Why

In addition to setting a good What, you have to know your Why. In fact, I can't overemphasize the importance of knowing your Why. Your Why is the secret to your success. If your Why is clear enough, you can harness its power to overcome any obstacle and never quit pursuing your What. You may have to take a breather now and then, but you'll never give up. If your Why isn't clear, however, you'll quickly find yourself doubting what you're doing. Growth and success and confidence and self-actualization require effort. Mountains of effort. If you have a weak Why, where are you going to pull from in order to build those mountains?

People frequently underestimate the importance of their Why because so many Whats in life come simply enough that a weak Why is sufficient to the task. These people then fall short when something truly worthwhile is on the table because those big-picture things don't come so easily. Don't believe me? Look at the rate of marriage failures or college dropouts around the country and the world. There are head-liner events (weddings and graduations) with whole lines of greeting cards dedicated to them, yet people often fail in the process or fail to maintain the results after making it through the first round.

It's ironic that this happens because the world of modern media and entertainment would have us believe that a worthwhile life is only the life spent saving the world. We watch all these acts of heroism "for the greater good," yet don't look to do anything heroic or even lesser good in our own lives. Why? Because people are out of tune with their Whys. People don't know Why they should be doing anything. We'll talk more about how to overcome this challenge, but remember that Why is extremely important. Without it, you'll be ill-equipped to reach your potential.

How

This part is probably easiest to understand. In order to get from where you are to where you want to be, you need to have a path. That path is your How. It's the method or concept or principle or whatever which will get you from where you are now to where you want to be. Your How can be just as detailed, complex, and structured as you need or as simple, abstract, and vague as you want. Your How is totally up to you, and it will be different from anyone else in the same situation.

Let's put that in perspective. If you and a friend are standing together in a grassy field and want to run to a tree in the distance, you'll both do it differently. First of all, you're standing beside each other, so you're starting in slightly different spots. Secondly, your strides are different because of a number of variables (muscle tone, leg length, gait and swing, etc.) so you'll take a different number of steps to traverse the field. Thirdly, your level of fitness is likely different, so you'll run at different speeds. Even if you run it as a race, one of you will outperform the other and reach the tree first.

There are a host of other reasons why you will both take different paths (air currents, terrain deformities, shoes and clothing, angle of the sun, mental preparedness, etc.), but you get the point. Even if you took turns, whoever went first would change the environment for the person who ran second. It's physically impossible for two people to run to that tree in exactly the same way.

Similarly, it's pretty much impossible for two people to get to the same What by exactly the same How. We can give each other principles and ideas and best practices, but in the end, your How has to be your own—even if that means adopting someone else's How and making it your own.

Harnessing Your Brain

Conveniently, What, Why, and How correlate fairly well with the different levels of your brain. What is largely a function of thought and choice corresponds nicely with your neocortex and rational thought. That's why it's so easy to come up with a long list of Whats. Your Why is housed deep down in the limbic brain. It's related to survival and the way that things will either improve or damage your chances for survival, ultimately deciding everything. Your How hangs around the midbrain. This is the part of your brain that looks at problems (how do I get from here to there) and works with your neocortex to come up with solutions.

Why does this matter to you?

Sadly, most people go about the goal-setting process backwards. Because they are so focused on getting the different "Whats" they want, they fail to ensure alignment between the neocortex and the limbic brain. This results in people's conscious minds having to do all the work and bear the entire load. The unmatched power of instinct and survival—alignment with your Why—is never brought to bear. This is like going to the championship game and benching your star players; it ruins your chances for victory.

The problem is that most people live and work solely in the neocortex. They go through their lives totally unaware of what goes on in the black box just under the surface. They never train the lion to work for them, and they never understand why sometimes it doesn't obey—which brings me to another point about your limbic brain. We talked about your neocortex being the logic center of your brain. Rational thought goes on there, but what about irrational thought? What about emotion?

You guessed it. The limbic brain—the decision center of the brain— is the place where emotion thrives. Your limbic brain is the source of your "gut impulses"—those things that don't make rational sense but feel right so you do them anyway. The limbic brain has no capacity for language, so it has no vehicle for logical debate. Instead, your limbic system identifies feelings (true or false), and latches on. At that point, your neocortex can argue all the logic it wants, but the limbic brain has already decided, and you're going along for the ride whether you like it or not.

In order to effectively harness your brain power, you need to learn how to tap into the limbic brain. You need to learn how to rally your emotions and all their raw power and then direct all of that energy and strength at the Whats of your life. In other words, you need to learn how to make your Why align with your What, or more accurately, you need to learn how to align your Whats in life with your Why—the limbic brain doesn't change so easily.

Thankfully, if you can learn how to align with your Why, you'll unleash a power within yourself that will drive you to accomplish things that you could hardly have dreamed of before. The journey won't have fewer steps than it would have had without your limbic brain working for you, but you'll have reserves of strength and will-power that you never could have imagined. It will make hard things become easier, or at least sustain you until you reach your goal.

How do you do align with your Why? I'm glad you asked.

Life is Like a Seesaw

Think back to when you were a child, when you were about seven years old or so. Imagine walking to that park you always loved to visit. You look around and see the monkey bars, the swings, the slides, and the seesaws. It's early on a fresh, Spring, Saturday morning. There's a touch of dew on the grass that the sun hasn't burned away yet, and no one else is here. The whole place is yours, so you take your time to play on each piece of playground equipment in sequence—until you reach the teeter-totter.

As you walk over, by yourself, you notice that the seesaw is sitting perfectly level. It's balanced to be nice and smooth across from one seat to the other, neither end higher than the other. Then you sit on it. The seat drops to the ground, slamming down into the mulch. You sit there for a minute looking way up at the other seat. With nothing at the other end, the seesaw is now seriously imbalanced, and it's a long way up to that other spot.

You hold on to the handle and jump a few times in an effort to push your seat up and bring the other seat down, but your weight inevitably brings you crashing back down to the mulch. No matter how hard you try, you can't simply muscle your way through. If you can't find a way to counterbalance that other seat, you'll be stuck sitting on the ground.

Now, would it surprise you if I told you that most things in life are a lot like this seesaw? Probably hard to see it, right? What if you imagine it on a huge scale? Like Indiana Jones big. We're talking a huge, wide beam that you can stand on—one with little handholds the whole way up to the other end—and the task you face is to climb to the other end. Your choice is to stay in the relative safety of where you are or to push forward and climb up and over—to the better life that awaits you.

Life is a lot like this dinosaur-sized teeter-totter in that you need to climb up and over challenges time and time again. That's a pretty intimidating task when the fulcrum (the hinge at the middle) is higher than a house. The good news is that, once you reach halfway, you're climbing down instead of up, right? Your weight and momentum will help carry you down. The catch is that you still need to climb down; you have to maintain control. If you simply let go and try to slide, you'll end up shooting off the bottom down into whatever lies below (in a real Indiana Jones movie, it would be a pit full of spikes—and snakes).

Riding a Bike

By now, you're probably wondering how this seesaw analogy can possibly apply to real life at all, much less apply to becoming the best you can be, so let me explain it in a basic sense, and then we'll dig into the different components so you can see how it all fits together with the levels of the brain we just talked about.

With any new task in life, there's a process you have to go through to get from start to finish. Traditionally, we talk about this as how you get from Point A to Point B. In reality, it's more like the How of getting from Point A to Point Z—without skipping any of the points in between. Bear with me for a moment as I suggest that every task requires a certain amount of effort and a certain amount of confidence. We'll talk more later about exactly what I mean by the term **confidence**, but let me lay this out for you so you can see what I mean.

Most people in most parts of the world can ride a bike. Not everyone can (and if you're one of the people who can't, I apologize), but most people can. How did that happen? It started with the person wanting to ride a bike for whatever reason. Once the desire grew bright enough, that person got on a bike and gave it a shot—and crashed. Now, for people without a strong Why, that first crash might have turned them off from ever trying again. For everyone else, their Why was strong enough to get them on that bike to try again. And again. Eventually, the concepts of rotational physics engage to help us stay upright and we learn to balance, steer, brake, and start. Almost like magic, we can ride a bike whenever we want. I've glossed over the time and effort and skinned knees, of course, but you get the idea.

The Belief Blueprint

Now, looking back at that learning process, let me introduce you to The Belief Blueprint. Do you remember that seesaw we were talking about a moment ago? Well, here's a visual explanation of what I was talking about.

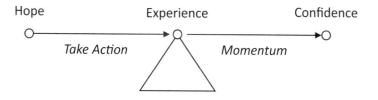

Here's how this works. Whenever you start something new, whether it's a new job or a new relationship or a new hobby or a new anything, you start at the left end of the model and sit down, just like little 7-year-old you on the seesaw all by yourself. And, just like it did in the story, you go crashing to the ground while the right-hand side sticks up into the air. This model represents the process of moving from where you are currently over to your What—where you want to go—and you'll notice that it becomes an uphill battle the moment you sit down. Not very promising, is it?

So let's dissect this in terms of learning to ride a bike. Initially, can you ride a bike? No. When you're just starting out you have only your Hope of being able to ride a bike. You have your desire, but you don't feel very confident in your ability yet (because you easily recognize that you have none). When you sit down, the weight of that doubt carries you down to the ground.

At that point, you can either sit there, stare up, and do nothing; or you can Take Action. How do you Take Action? You get on the bike and start carefully pedaling. Maybe you even start smaller by using a bike with training wheels. Either way, you Take Action and start doing things that should bring you closer to the goal of being able to ride a bike. Maybe you read a book about rotational physics and how a bike doesn't want to fall over once it gets going. Maybe you watch a movie about riding a bike. You could take a class about bike safety. All of those things are good, but nothing will replace the act of simply getting on your bike and going for it.

You'll fall a number of times, but you are gaining Experience each time you do. Initially, that might be things like "Turn right out of the driveway because the Johnsons parked their car funny and I'll crash into it if I go left" or "I need to avoid that pothole or I'll bend another rim and break another helmet." Eventually, your insights will change from hard facts to more conceptual things like "I need to keep my head up and stay alert or things can jump out at me before I have time to react—like the neighbor's cat" or "I need to hit that hill with some speed or I'll slow down too much, get tired, and fall over."

As you gain this Experience, you are shifting from the left to the right along that seesaw, closing in on the center point—the balance point. Once you have enough Experience to reach that center point, a beautiful thing happens. By shifting your weight from the one side to the other, you will tip the seesaw over to the other side. This means that you now have a downhill journey to reach your goal. What used to feel so high up out of reach is now right in front of you and totally doable. The Momentum you've built through gaining those Experiences will make the rest of the path feel much easier.

Ultimately, the weight of your Experience and the Momentum you've developed will push you through to the right-hand side. You'll reach the point of Confidence on the model. At that point, you have Confidence that you can ride a bike without falling. And the best part? Once you've fought for the results and obtained Confidence, it's yours forever. No one can take your skills and knowledge from you. At that point, you can transfer your newfound Confidence into working on a new What—like riding a motorcycle.

Connecting Your Brain

We'll get into the nitty-gritty of the model in the rest of the book, but first I wanted to make a few connections for you. You may or may not have caught on to a few terms I used as I was describing the process of moving from your initial Hope or Desire all the way to your final goal of Confidence. Either way, I'm going to pull them out now and show you how they relate to what we've already been discussing.

First, your Why is your Hope or Desire. This is the inner force, an unmet core need that causes you to dream up a number of goals you'd like to reach for. It becomes your reason to believe that you can ever make it up that initial incline. Let's simplify things for a moment starting with your Why. We'll call this Point A.

●

Point A—Why

Next, the What part of the model is obvious. This is the end goal, or the thing in which you want Confidence, and it's designated by the neocortex. We'll call this Point B. Once both points are established, just like a Cartesian plane, you suddenly have a trajectory. This is the direction of where you're applying your efforts and the victory you're fighting for.

●————————————————————●

Point A—Why   Point B—What

Last, the How segment is where the magic happens. This is the part of the diagram where you Take Action to gain Experience in order to build Momentum, the means by which over time you tip the odds in your favor and eventually get to where you want to be. This is the problem-solving and adaptation part of the process that relies on your midbrain.

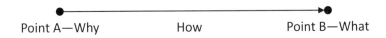

Point A—Why   How   Point B—What

Your Why will determine whether or not you have enough strength to make it that far. This is why it's so critical to get your limbic brain behind you. You need to have a deep, powerful Why to trigger that emotional powerhouse to carry you through until you have Confidence. At that point, your confidence and that deep Why will connect to make you unstoppable in that thing. You will have trained the lion.

To continue progressing in life, simply repeat the process on each and every new challenge and opportunity you face. As you do so, your overall confidence will grow, your understanding of your limbic brain will increase, and your power to accomplish what you want will go through the roof. You'll turn into one of those people I mentioned in the introduction—the kind of person who seems to have success in everything, time and time again.

Start With Hope

But there's a caution here. You have to work toward your end goal, toward Confidence, but you certainly won't start there. You can't start at the end. You have to start with Hope. Even if you can't do anything stronger than just *want* to believe that you can one day have the Confidence, that's where you have to start.

You can't start anywhere else because you won't be able to force that lion to do what you want after the fact. If you choose an objective that the limbic brain disagrees with, you will just be setting yourself up for failure. You'll be setting up a conflict between your neocortex and the lion—and that's not a battle you want to see. I'll give you a hint about how it ends: the survival instinct is amazingly strong.

So, with that in mind, we're going to dig into your Why. We're going to start with Hope. If you want to reach your potential and be your best, you need to have your limbic brain working for you. You, as the trainer, need to learn how to work with the lion. If you can do just that one thing, you'll be able to put on a show that most people can't even dream of—and we're not going to stop there. In any case, let's get started with Hope.

HOPE

Hope

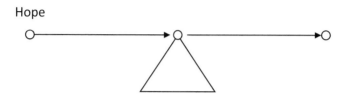

Hope - [hohp]
- n. - the feeling that what is wanted can be had or that events will turn out for the best
- v.t. - to look forward to with desire and reasonable confidence
- v.i. - to feel that something desired may happen[1]

What is Hope? As you can see from the definitions above, hope can be both a noun and a verb. Hope is a thing unto itself, but it's also an action. That's very fitting for our purposes because you need to be able to have Hope, but you also need to Hope your way into a better life through Taking Action.

Hope v. Belief

As we get into an explanation of Hope and what it means to you, there's something we need to clear up first. Hope is not Belief. Hope, as you just read, is a *feeling*. Feelings are the domain and currency of the limbic brain, your emotional center. The limbic brain has no capacity for

---

[1] hope. Dictionary.com.*Dictionary.com Unabridged.* Random House, Inc. http://dictionary.reference. com/browse/hope (accessed: January 28, 2015).

description, logic, language, or rationalization. Instead, the limbic brain communicates up to your neocortex in feelings, which you then have to attempt to define and translate into words. Talk about a communication barrier.

The neocortex, however, has full grasp of language and standard forms of communication. It's your thought center. Haven't you ever argued with yourself about something before? Belief is a form of thought. Belief is a "logical" decision to treat something as true, typically based on some form of evidence (though that evidence is often in the form of feelings). It is "an opinion or conviction"[2] and conviction is a form of convince (i.e., to be convinced), or "to move by argument or evidence."[3]

The limbic brain, on the other hand, has no capacity for argument or evidence. The limbic brain can't be "convinced" of things through logical discussion. Things either *feel* right, or they don't. Your feelings can change over time, but they generally change in relation to experiences you have, not discussions going on between your ears. When was the last time you "convinced" yourself to not be mad or scared or happy? You can't convince emotions to change without providing an experiential input. Evidence and argument are language-based, outside-brain tools. Belief, therefore, is also a capacity of the neocortex, but it frequently relies on feelings as "evidence." In this way, Belief serves as a bridge between thought and feeling, or the neocortex and limbic brain.

In fact, this is where we get the concept of heart and mind from. The mind, or belief, is the neocortex. This is the logic mechanism of the brain. Something makes sense for whatever reason (reason is another indicator of neocortex activity; emotions need no reason), and that's comforting to us in our upper-level, logic-brain existence. The traditional view of the heart, on the other hand, isn't remotely related to that bundle of muscle beating in your chest. The only feeling your physical heart is capable of is pain, and that generally manifests in the left arm or up in your jaw for reasons of physiological development and embry-

---

[2] belief. Dictionary.com. *Dictionary.com Unabridged*. Random House, Inc. http://dictionary.reference.com/browse/belief (accessed: January 28, 2015).

[3] convinced. Dictionary.com. *Dictionary.com Unabridged*. Random House, Inc. http://dictionary.reference.com/browse/convinced (accessed: January 28, 2015).

ology that we won't get into here. The "heart," in the sense of heart and mind, is the center of feelings and gut impulses. Where do we have feelings? You've got it—the limbic brain.

With that in mind, I will be referring to both Hope and Belief independently throughout the remainder of this book. I may, however, also refer to them in the aggregate at times. If I do, I will use the term Hope and move on. In terms of what we're working toward, your Hope is the key to your success anyway. Once you can activate your Hope, the Belief will come along in time to bridge your thoughts to your Hopes. Hope, after all, is where the real power comes from. Your limbic brain runs 24/7 to monitor and control your entire body. Comparatively, your neocortex runs for a few hours a day before needing to defragment and reboot by sleeping. Your neocortex couldn't even lift a finger if the limbic brain didn't let it. To help you see this relationship, I'm going to share with you a true story.

Hopes and "Other Things"

America has often been called the Land of Opportunity, or even the Land of Dreams, but that doesn't mean that the country has always been optimistic and hopeful. In the early 1960s, public sentiment was that the USSR was winning the space race. In other words, communism was beating capitalism. As you can imagine, Hope was running a bit thin. The country needed a jumpstart to re-engage the collective limbic brain and re-energize.

In response to that need, a speech was given on September 12, 1962. The speech listed a history of the victories the country had achieved in the past—with an emphasis on scientific and peaceful victories—and then issued a challenge. I'll quote just a portion of the speech here.

Up to that point, President John F. Kennedy had been talking about problems and history that everyone already knew about. He was speaking to a shared experience and reality. He was expressing a common sentiment, but the crowd hadn't fully connected yet. He was operating in the realm of What, in the neocortex land of words and language and logical argument. He was sharing beliefs. There's a lot to be gained from verbal discourse (as we'll demonstrate later), but JFK was talking to people who agreed with him. These people didn't need the kind of convincing that comes through logic and rhetoric; they already understood.

Have you heard the expression "shoot for the moon" before? That's exactly what JFK decided to do. When he issued his challenge, the nature of his speech changed. I'll share here the most-quoted portion so you can see what I mean: "We choose to go to the moon. We choose to go to the moon in this decade and do the *other things*, not because they are easy, but because they are hard, because that goal will serve to organize and measure the best of our energies and skills, because that challenge is one that we are willing to accept, one we are unwilling to postpone, and one which we intend to win, and *the others*, too."

What are "the other things"? Turns out, he was referencing past achievements of climbing mountains and flying across the Atlantic. He called them "other things" because they weren't important. What was important was that people needed to understand the Why. He'd given them the What, and now he was helping them to engage with it. He was giving them Hope.

That's the power of Hope. Hope is Why. Hope is seated deep in the limbic brain and it stirs the emotions, rallying their power. Hope isn't about words because words are the domain of the neocortex. Hope is about the gut, about deeper motivation and aspirations. Hope communicates to the deepest corners of the heart, not the mind, and therein lies the power. That's where the power of JFK's speech came from. He wasn't just using words to attempt to persuade people, he was showing them his Hope—his Why—and enabling them to make it their own. He was trying to rally people to rise up, to harness their own Hope to make themselves better—and then work to make America the Land of Dreams again. Why? To make the world a better, safer place.

Velocity

So, what is Hope? As with JFK, Hope is your Why. It's the power that drives you to do and be more. Hope is your *desire* to be more. Hope is your expectation that your desire can turn into reality, that your unmet need will be fulfilled. The strength of your Hope will largely determine how committed you are to whatever course of action you need to take. If you have high hopes, you'll be willing to put more on the line to see the process through from start to finish. If your hopes are weak, you won't be willing to risk as much on them. You might still reach the finish, but it will take far more time to aggregate the required effort. Hope is velocity.

There's an interesting thing about velocity. People think that speed and velocity are the same, but that's only because those people haven't studied physics. Speed tells us the distance an object travels in a certain amount of time; e.g., "mph" stands for miles per hour or distance (miles) per unit of time (hour). Speed, however, is a relatively useless term because it misses a key element. If I tell you that I'm driving at 60 mph, what do you know? Only the rate at which I'm traveling. In one hour, I'll be 60 miles farther along, but you don't know where I'm heading. I could be driving in a circle for all you know!

Velocity adds this other, critical element to the picture: direction. In order to have a velocity, you need to know the speed something is traveling *and* the direction it's going. Speed alone isn't enough. Everyone can move quickly when they need to. That's the power of the limbic brain. The survival instinct (the fight or flight response) is rooted in millennia of development. Your neocortex has only been building itself for a few weeks before you were born. The neocortex basically comes as a blank slate. The limbic brain comes preloaded with all kinds of powerful survival software. It can rally a person and make that person move in ways that would stun bystanders, but the limbic brain likes to pick its own direction. The limbic brain largely determines velocity—Hope—so you need to make sure that it's in line with where your neocortex thinks you want to go.

So let's talk about that process. How do you get your limbic brain to bring your Why on board and in line with your What? As we've said before, you don't. You bring your What in line with your Why—which means you need to know your Why, right? Once you know your Why, you can learn how to apply it to any number of different Whats with the same, stunning results. In other words, as long as you know your Point A, any Point B you set will be in harmony, and the level of Hope you bring will equal the velocity at which you progress.

Finding Why

Finding your Why isn't an overly complex process, but it's a bit more involved than simply asking "Why do you want that?" There's a lot more to a person's Why than we typically think. It goes deeper than you can imagine, and that's the reason it carries so much weight and power. Beliefs can change on what feels like a daily basis, all depending on the information you receive, but your deepest Hopes run deep and don't change often at all. The good news is that—because Hopes don't change often and usually do so only by small degrees—once you figure out your Why, you can count on it not changing anytime soon.

To find your true Why, you first have to understand that you won't really be able to use words to explain it at first. Because your true Why lives in your limbic brain, it will be based on feelings and impulses, not rational thought and words. It won't come out like the lovely mission statement you put up on the wall for everyone to admire. Instead, it'll feel like a piece of you, and it may be far too personal for you to want to display it to everyone.

Additionally, keep in mind that the limbic brain is the brain of instinct and survival, not the brain of altruism and self-sacrifice. For the limbic brain, the needs of the group probably don't outweigh the needs of the one. In the wild, it's kill or be killed. Animals don't generally go out of their way to help other animals—not even animals of the same species. In fact, many animal species will turn cannibalistic when food is scarce. Some, like grizzly bears, will even kill and eat their own babies rather than run the risk of having those babies grow up to become competition in the future. I promise that the limbic brain has your best interests in mind at all times, but you might not recognize it that way at first. Emotions aren't always a pretty thing. What you find will, at first, probably seem surprisingly self-serving. That's normal, and it doesn't mean you're an egomaniac or a bad person. In fact, to demonstrate this point to you, let me relate a story of a time I went through this process with a lady where I work.

Deep Diving

There was a lady on a team I managed who just didn't quite seem to perform to her full potential. She mostly got her job done, but she had so much untapped ability and just wasn't thriving. Other managers in the company had talked to her and worked with her, but she just wasn't making much progress. Finally, I took a turn to mentor her. She'd already been through several goal-setting sessions and she had plenty of resources at her disposal, so I had to take a different approach. In so doing, I stumbled on this technique to help unlock the Why behind a person's actions.

We sat down and talked about how things were going. After we got through the pleasantries, we started talking a little more seriously about her level of engagement with what she was doing. This happened a number of years ago, so I don't remember the actual words, but I'm going to walk you through our conversation so you can see how it all happened.

As I said, she'd done all the preparatory goal setting and everything else that everyone had recommended, but she was still hitting walls. In spite of that, she hadn't quit. She kept coming back, and I knew there had to be a reason, so I asked her. I asked her why she was even there working in that business. I don't remember what she told me initially, but I knew right away that it wasn't the truth. It was what she'd been telling herself and it sounded really nice as a mission statement, but it wasn't Why she was working in the business.

So I took it a step further. I listened to the weak answer she gave me and then asked, "And why is that important to you?" She thought about it and answered, and I responded again, "Why does that matter to you?" We went the rounds with this several times. She'd give me an answer, and I'd ask her why that answer mattered. Why did she care? What we didn't really know at the time is that she was digging down into her limbic brain, down into her core, to answer me. Every question and subsequent answer peeled away one more layer of the onion. Eventually, we reached a point where she was crying—a great indicator that she was in the limbic, emotional brain. Finally, we'd reached that level where she was really tapped into what truly drove her.

Now, I'd taken her through that exercise out of frustration more than anything. She wouldn't walk away, but she wasn't helping the team either. I think, to an extent, I was trying to get her to decide to stay or go. Thankfully she didn't quit. Instead, we went on a journey together that opened her mind to her Why and gave her the motivation she needed to make some real progress. She left that meeting with a level of clarity that I don't think she'd ever had before. I left that meeting wondering exactly what I'd done and how I could replicate it with others. In fact, I spent a lot of time in the following months and years testing things out in order to develop the process I use today.

Can you see how things worked? We started at a high-level, verbal, rational, wonderful, frame-it-and-put-it-on-the-wall level and then progressed down through the abstract impressions of the midbrain into a place where she couldn't even speak. It took her time to sort through the emotions of what she *felt* before she could wrap crude words around a deep, personal knowledge. More importantly, do you see how what she initially perceived to be her Why was actually very different from her *real* Why? At the same time, do you see how they are related? How her first answer was a hollow, neocortex translation of what was really going on deep beneath the surface? It just got twisted a bit on the way up. Her true feelings were lost in translation.

Once she realized her true Why, she learned how to tap into that emotional power. It didn't take long before she was progressing again. Her performance didn't explode over night, but you could see her steady improvement from there. Knowing your true Why—your Core Why—will help you achieve a new level of steady, never-ending improvement. You might not move any faster than before, but you'll feel greater purpose in the journey. You'll move forward with dogged consistency, and nothing will be able to stop you.

With all that said, let's start the process of finding your Core Why. Once we get through, we can talk more about how these things come together and make sense—and how you can use a seemingly selfish Why to do the most amazing selfless acts.

Preparation

Preparing for this exercise, you must think of a goal you have. I know that seems totally out of line with everything I've been saying so far, but bear with me. Just like with this coworker of mine, you can't just jump straight into the limbic brain. It wouldn't make any sense to your rational mind. Instead, we have to back into it and set up a shared frame of reference between your neocortex and your limbic brain. We have to bridge hope and belief and create a moment of unity in order to find clarity.

So, again, think of what you want. Think of a goal. Make it something that you already feel an emotional push to strive for—even if your mind isn't necessarily on board yet. Choose a goal that you already have an emotional connection to. You need to feel that your Why is in place even if you don't understand your Why yet. This could be a job you're pursuing (like the woman in the example) or a relationship you're developing. Typically, thinking about a fancy sports car or some other material desire isn't as effective, but you're welcome to give it a go and see what happens.

Do you have that goal in mind? Good. You're now ready to begin.

Step One

Get a blank sheet of paper and a pen. You might also choose to use the blank notes pages at the back of the book. Whatever you do just be sure to write your answers down by hand. The simple action of putting pen to paper fires tens of thousands more neurons in your brain than typing, allowing more connections to be made and more honest and pure information to flow.

Now that you have your goal in mind, I want you to ask yourself a question. Just as you saw in the example above, the next several steps will involve questions as you move deeper into your limbic brain. So, let's go over a couple ground rules. You're *trying* to get down to your limbic brain now. Does your limbic brain operate in logical analyses or Boolean scripts (true/false, if/then type stuff used in computer programming)? No. It doesn't. It operates in gut impulses and feelings. It can't be reasoned with, and it reacts very quickly (a moment of indecision and the lion will have already overpowered you). You have to let your guard down. Let go of any preconceived ideas of what you *think* the right answer is. Follow what you *feel*.

Also, in order to help you make that transition from neocortex down to the limbic brain, I'm going to prompt your answers for you. I will ask a question and give you the first couple words of your answer. Initially, the answers won't be too hard, but that will change as we move deeper. No matter how difficult it gets, though, I want you to fill in the rest of the answer as quickly as you can. Remember, your limbic brain won't sit and ponder about this. It will act on a quick gut reaction. If you find yourself sitting and thinking for very long, you've probably already ignored the input from your limbic brain and turned back to your neocortex for answers. Each step should take no more than 30 seconds to a minute to complete. Don't wander back up into the neocortex. Does that make sense?

Okay. We'll be starting out in your neocortex and moving down, so the first few answers may translate into words quite easily. That's normal. Ready? Get your goal back in mind. Now, the question—and make sure to write down your answer somewhere.

Q. Why are you pursuing this goal?

A. *Because I...*

Step Two

Let's take a look at the answer you just wrote down. If you're like most people, your answer was something that sounds great in public. It's well thought out and impressive to people like you. It probably incorporates elements of helping others or doing something for the greater good (unless you're thinking about that sports car). That's okay. That's normal at this level. We're still basically in your neocortex, so the answer should sound good.

Most companies and individuals, by the way, stop here when they're creating a mission statement. I have to admit that there's a strong temptation to stop here. This answer was fairly easy to get and it fits so perfectly with the focus and direction of your neocortex. It's easy for you to understand and it sounds so great to you and others.

It would look good on a wall, t-shirt, or bumper sticker. But that's the catch. It *looks* and *sounds* great, but does it accurately represent your deepest *feelings*?

This will all change as we move down. As we go, your answers will get progressively harder to put into words—yet progressively more powerful and personal to you. You will shift from things that look and sound good to things that *feel* right. So let's continue. Go back and reread what you wrote down in Step One. Do you have it in your mind? Good. Next question.

Q. **Looking at your answer above, why is that important to you?**

A. *Because I think...*

Step Three

Make sure to write down your answer again. You can always shred it when we're done, but I think you'll want to keep it. In either case, do you see how we're still working in the neocortex? By prompting you to record what you *think*, I'm keeping you in your neocortex, but I'm pushing you deeper by making you justify your first answer. You may have felt some emotional stirrings as this second answer puts us at the doorway to your limbic brain. Keep that answer close at hand because you'll need it for this next question.

Q. **Looking at your answer above, why is that important to you?**

A. *Because I believe...*

Step Four

Are you starting to feel the shift we're making? We've gone from what you think to what you believe. You are probably feeling some emotion as we move closer to the limbic brain and you might be struggling to write down something more than platitudes, affirmations, or seemingly random beliefs. This is the fun part where we try to leave logic behind. If you're struggling to make sense of it, just keep moving into the next step.

Before you write your answer to Step Four, I need to remind you that your Why is not about anyone or anything else but you. You may have spent a good part of your life serving others—a spouse or partner, children, and others. Parental service, particularly that of mothers, has a way of wearing away awareness of personal needs over time, substituting the well-being of your loved ones and dependents for your own. "If they're happy, I'm happy," you tell yourself. Many people struggle at this step in the process and begin to feel terribly selfish as they dive deeper into their own needs. Maslow's Hierarchy of Needs, which we'll reference more later, affirms that everything we do is to serve a basic human need. Even the seemingly altruistic and charitable things we do are fueled by the need to be safe or to feel important. You must strip away the habitual outward focus, and look inward right now in order to get to your Core Why. Now let's take another step down. Make sure you're writing down what you can. This next one might be difficult.

Q. Looking at your answer above, how do you know this?

A. *Because I know...*

If you're struggling to articulate an answer here, you may want to describe *how* you came to know what you know. We can only know the light if we have known darkness, sweet if we have experienced bitter, and so on. The experiences that have shaped your limbic responses to this point could have happened in your formative childhood or teenage years, or maybe more recently. Whatever it is, you have significant pivotal moments in your past that will surface at this point and provide a foundation for why you do what you do.

Conclusion

Feel free to take a moment here at this final step. Most people struggle to articulate this part. I'm asking what they know, yet they can't really describe it. Sometimes it's a moment of panic, but it's almost always a moment of intense insight. If you have trouble putting it into words, don't worry. You're not alone. Most people struggle with that, and it's a good thing. The limbic brain doesn't operate in words. It operates in feelings and emotions.

Look through what you wrote down in Step Four and search for a key word, phrase, or mental image that best articulates the feelings you're experiencing right now. If nothing is jumping out at you quite yet, that doesn't mean you haven't landed on it. If you've reached a point where your feelings seem to overpower your words, then you've most likely arrived. If you're not sure, you can always ask the question in Step Four again and again—as often as needed. Each time you ask yourself those "Why is that important/How do you know" kinds of questions, you drive yourself deeper inside. The deeper you go, the more primal things will get. Eventually, you'll connect with your true Why. Now that you have your Why, make sure to record it somewhere and keep it safe. As I said before, it may evolve over time, and you can certainly train your limbic brain to point that Why in some amazing directions, but your Core Why won't really change much like your What might. The limbic brain doesn't jump around like the neocortex.

Finding Your Why Exercise

For those of you who didn't do the exercise with me a moment ago (or for whom the exercise didn't work as well due to the breaks in between questions to discuss things), I've included it again here without any of the explanations or interjections. Please, before you proceed with the book, make sure to take a moment and do this exercise. It's not only enlightening, it's essential. You *need* to know your Core Why or the rest of what I'm going to teach you will be almost useless. From here out, I'll be operating under the assumption that you know your Why, and the material will make the most sense if you can apply it in that light.

So, for those of you who need to run through it again, here it is. Take as long as you need, and feel free to run through the questions multiple times. You can also add a few more why questions at the end if you feel the need to dig deeper. Eventually, there just won't be an answer, but you'll be so far beyond words that you won't even be able to express fully what you're feeling. Your Why will be a step or so ahead of that point. Also, for those of you who think this would be useful for others and want to take them through it, this will likely be the easier spot to reference. Just make sure to give that other person a few minutes to answer each question before asking the next question.

Prep: Think of your goal (a job or relationship works best, but a material thing can do in a pinch so long as it's in goal form)

Q. Why are you pursuing this goal?
A. *Because I...*

Q. Looking at your answer above, why is that important to you?
A. *Because I think...*

Q. Looking at your answer above, why is that important to you?
A. *Because I believe...*

Q. Looking at your answer above, how do you *know* this?
A. *Because I know...*

At this point, emotions should be running high. If they aren't, go back to question four and ask the last two questions over and over again as many times as necessary to get to that speechless, emotional state. That's the destination, and it should feel like you're opening up that deep, dark place way down inside—only to find light and direction there.

This whole process is designed to take you down through the layers of your brain to find your Core Why, your True Why. So let's talk about the different things you discovered on the way down, then we'll talk about your Core Why itself.

In Step One you stated why you're pursuing your goal. I mean no offense, and at this point you understand, but I refer to this as the Fake Why because it fakes people out. They *think* it's their Why, but that's exactly the problem. They're still *thinking* about it instead of *feeling* it. So many other Why exercises out there focus on all these external factors instead of getting to the *real core* of what makes us tick. The Fake Why resides in the neocortex and provides only very limited motivation, no matter how great these surface answers sound. Next, as we move down, we pass through the cognitive levels of your brain. This leads us to the next segment, the belief system which bridges the gap between neocortex and limbic brain through the midbrain—if we let it. Many people ignore their belief system whenever it proves inconvenient to the task at hand—reinforcing the delusion of control they have in their neocortex.

Once you break down the articulations of your belief system, you can finally get access to the feelings that influence those beliefs. It's like being granted access to your own private library of thoughts, feelings, and memories. You can dig down into the volumes of "evidence" that support your belief system. You can read all about your limbic brain and explore the feelings that shape your own True Why—your Core Why. Interestingly, because so many people spend their lives outside in the neocortex, the True Why can sometimes seem almost foreign even at the same time that it reflects a person's deepest feelings. Let's talk about your Core Why now.

Debrief

First, take a deep breath and calm yourself. Then go back and reread your Core Why. Is it enlightening at all? Is it alarming? As I warned you before, many people are surprised by how self-centric their Why is. Let me soothe your fears about that a bit. I'm going to get into something that some people might find almost heretical here (especially for those of you who are religious, like me), so bear with me. Hear me out until the end before you decide whether what I'm saying rings true or not.

Your Core Why has to be self-centric. That's actually a good thing. After all, your decision center in your brain—the limbic brain—also drives the survival instinct. If you're faced with a decision from which you benefit in absolutely no way, shape, or form, a normal limbic brain is going to write off that decision and walk away. There's no benefit for the limbic brain to weigh against the expense of time and effort, there's no improvement of survival odds. If your Core Why were truly altruistic, it would mean that you literally spent your days helping others at the expense of yourself. You would value service to others (or whatever else your Core Why indicates) on a higher level than the basic necessities of life. I hope I don't have to point out that a value system like that would be very detrimental to your health and wellness.

Now, this sounds cold, but let me break it down for you. Not everything comes down to getting food, water, or shelter. When you help someone else, you can nurture positive feelings inside yourself. This is the warmth you get from doing service. Not only that, but you need to make sure that you're in your best shape in order to do the most good for others. If you aren't taking care of yourself, how can you really expect to take care of someone (or something) else?

This is the reason that, in the case of an emergency during a flight such as a loss of cabin pressure, the airline attendants always instruct you to put on your own oxygen mask first. If you don't take care of yourself first, how can you expect to be at your best when you try to help others? In the case of the oxygen mask, you need to make sure you can breathe and survive in order to be around to help your children. It doesn't do you a lot of good to get your child or elderly seat mate taken care of if you then pass out and die. Who's going to take care of that person now? What if you didn't get the mask on quite right and it pops off? Who will put it back on the person?

Or what about a lifeguard? If the lifeguard jumps into the pool to save a drowning person and then values that other person more than he values himself, he'll hoist that other person above the water even at the expense of trapping himself below the surface. How can he effectively swim that person to the edge if he drowns first? Now there are two drowning people in the pool and the situation is actually worse than before.

Maslow's Hierarchy of Needs

To help you understand this system of needs and how the limbic brain prioritizes things, let's look at some research into simple behavioral psychology. As I said before, we're going to look a bit more at the

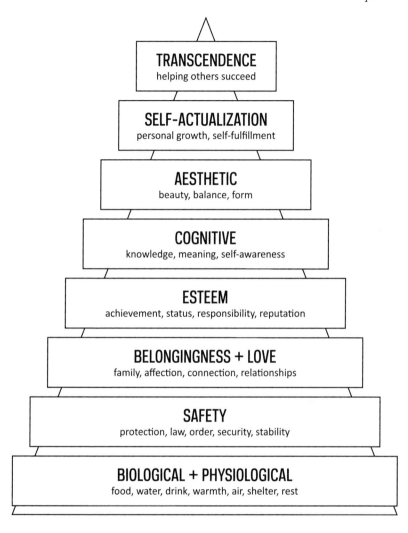

work of Abraham Maslow and an expanded version I like based on his Hierarchy of Needs.

This is, according to modern psychology, basically the order by which the limbic brain prioritizes things in life. It starts at the bottom of the pyramid and works its way up as the lower needs are met. Now, of course, you can skip a meal or two in favor of helping someone else. The Hierarchy never indicates that you can't. It's not until you've avoided your need for food for some time before it begins to assert itself. The same goes for any need on the pyramid. The hierarchy can be flexible that way.

Still, as a general rule, your gut impulses will lead you to take care of the more basic needs before backing off and allowing you to take care of the higher-level needs. In fact, as you take care of the lower-level things, the higher-level needs will become priorities for the limbic brain, and it will begin to push for you to meet those needs as well. That's why successful people tend to start to look for ways to influence others. They have learned how to fulfill their own needs and now desire to help others meet theirs too. As it turns out, this is just another reason why your Core Why needs to be self-focused. What better way to harness the power of the survival instinct for good things?

My paternal grandfather was a renowned ophthalmologist who spent his career studying his craft and improving his ability to serve others. After years of helping people regain their sight, he was often heard to say that, in effect, serving others is actually very selfish. We may be giving our time and resources, but we gain more in return than we have given. Can you see how moving from physiological needs on up to self-actualization is actually a journey of starting inward and working outward? By the top of the pyramid, almost everything you do benefits others while also benefiting you. This is why you can get your limbic, survival-instinct brain on board with the even most altruistic, self-sacrificing causes on the planet—once you understand how it ticks. Ultimately, helping others is as much a need as anything else; you just have to take care of your own basic needs first as that is where most of us start.

A caution here as you gauge your own starting point as well as that of the people with whom you work. I have worked with millionaires who are still struggling to fulfill basic levels of health, love, and esteem. I have also worked with people with few material possessions who are already reaching for self-actualization. Don't use monetary success or failure as a way to gauge where someone may fall on the hierarchy of needs. Your internal lion will demand compliance at some point.

So hang on to your Core Why. It's your starting place for How you are going to get to every What you choose to pursue in life. As long as you can use your powers of logic and reason to align your Whats with your Why, your limbic brain will come along willingly.

Opposites

Now that you know your Core Why, you're ready to see how it fits into The Belief Blueprint to help you build experience, train your limbic brain, and achieve more than you thought possible. First, though, it's also instructive to look at some opposites. It's a fact of life that we face challenges and resistance in just about everything we do. You could almost say that you face opposition in everything. If you didn't, you wouldn't need to read this book—or any other. Some people call it Karma; some people call it inertia; some people call it an act of God or an act of the Devil; some people just call it Murphy's Law. Whatever you call it, the fact remains that there are opposites to every positive thing in life.

Life and death, happiness and misery, health and sickness, love and hate, abundance and lack, and so on. We could go on naming these pairs all day, but we won't. We're going to focus on just a couple pairs which are important to note. These are the pairs of Hope with Despair and Belief with Doubt.

Hope, as you know, is your Core Why. Hope is at the heart of the feelings that motivate you to seek out something greater in life. As such, Hope provides the force behind your forward movement. Despair, however, is the opposite of Hope. It literally means the "loss of hope."[4] Despair is the acceptance of the idea that your Hope is impossible— that it can never come true. Despair means that you're letting go of your Why; you're giving up on it. Despair is the weight that drags you down.

When you feel Despair, you have let go of your Hope. This can be because you have decided that your What is too difficult—which really means that your Hope isn't strong enough—or because you simply never found your Core Why. Either way, your trainer is inter- fering with the lion. Your neocortex is getting in the way of your limbic brain. The result, Despair, is a powerful emotional response that will rip the energy out of you. It's the lion's way of showing you that you're ignoring it, and it will prove who is boss. There's no faster way to fail

---

[4] despair. Dictionary.com.*Dictionary.com Unabridged*. Random House, Inc. http://dictionary.refer- ence.com/browse/despair (accessed: January 28, 2015).

forever than to give up. In fact, I can't think of another way to fail forever at all. Everyone suffers setbacks in the long push forward, but as long as you're working toward fulfilling your true Why, you can't really fail until you quit.

To "decide" that your Hope isn't strong enough and that your neocortex can somehow do things on its own is like the trainer deciding it doesn't need the lion anymore. That might sound nice, but the trainer and the lion still have to share the same room—live in the same brain. How are you going to ignore that lion day after day? That is not an illusion of control anymore; it's a *delusion*. That's where Despair comes from. It comes from trying to fool yourself yet knowing, deep down, that you're living a lie.

Similarly, Doubt is the opposite of Belief. In order to climb the house-sized seesaw, you need to believe that you can make it in order for your neocortex to accept the support of your limbic brain. That Belief wraps up your Hope like the harness of a thoroughbred. It's the act of aligning your What with your Why. Doubt is just the opposite. Doubt is questioning your What in the same vein as Despair being denial of your Why. Doubt unlocks the power of *negative* thinking—the bane of success.

Doubt disengages your neocortex from the process, robbing the limbic brain of that much-needed direction. Worse still, it puts your neocortex in opposition with your limbic brain, setting you up to ultimately feel Despair. Typically, doubts come when we listen to outside forces. If we believe in something enough to start out on a journey toward that thing, it's usually some outside event that distracts us and causes us to lose vision. At that point, we run the risk of grabbing hold of something other than our Why to motivate us again. We usually turn to temporal motivators—things that don't last and don't meet our core needs. Since nothing else has the power to get us to push through the hard times, grabbing hold of something else actually weakens us. That's when the Doubts creep in—whispers of "What Ifs" in our ears. If we listen to our Doubts, we undermine our Belief and begin to derail the whole system.

Often, those Doubts come from within. We start to tell ourselves that we're not strong enough. We start to focus on the pain of the present moment rather than the ultimate victory of the What and the unbeatable strength of the Why. Sometimes, however, those Doubts don't come from within. Sometimes, they come from the people around us. Often, it's just society in general playing its defeatist games. Other times—worse times—it's the people closest to us who speak Doubt in our ears.

Opposition

You'll see increasing opposition as you start to accelerate your self-actualization and personal development illustrated in the Belief Blueprint. The faster you move, the more resistance you'll see from the people around you. In physics, you can look at this as the wind resistance against the windshield of a car. When the car is simply driving around town, the pressure against the glass is comparatively low. As the car accelerates to highway speeds, however, that resistance goes up. The car has to cut through the same density of air, but it has to make the cut at a much higher speed, making the oppositional force that much stronger.

The incremental increase in effort may not be as much, because you'll have Momentum and Experience on your side (more on those later), but the overall effort will still increase as you pick up Velocity. As you move at a faster and faster rate, people around you who don't share the same vision will be more likely to notice—and more likely to say something—because your movement requires them to change their perception of you and possibly even themselves. Most people, hopefully, will be supportive of you. Never underestimate the power of positive feedback. Never blow it off.

When people are supportive of you, when they're encouraging, be sure to thank them. Also be sure to acknowledge that feedback to yourself. By giving you positive feedback, those people are confirming your chosen trajectory. They are approving of your path. If they are people you love and respect, then you can take that as a vote of confidence—a vote of *Confidence*. Let that increase your Belief and reinforce your commitment to your Hope, your true Why.

Unfortunately, people won't always be supportive. For whatever reason, many people choose to ignore their own Why in life. I would guess that most of them don't even really know what their Why is. One of my favorite sayings, possibly a Chinese proverb, is "Inspiration without expression is depression." People who live life with their goals in opposition to their Why will feel an inner turmoil that they can't explain away, and it will drag them down and hold them back until they can get in line. People depressed in this way often give in and stop fighting altogether—in a way, they embrace Despair.

At that point, their depression becomes complete. It becomes a part of their being, something they will never escape on their own. The lion itself lies down and stops roaring for change. They can still come around by finding their Why and pursuing it, but they will need help to get that far. Until that time, they often look around in bitterness and jealousy at anyone who starts to show promise—at people like you.

What to Do

When this happens, try not to take it personally. It's not that those people have anything against you personally. They're actually often experiencing some level of depression over their own failure to find and align with their Why. You just happen to be a convenient target on which to take out that frustration. All the same, be ready for it because it will come. People may start to call you names or talk about you behind your back. When that happens, simply ignore it. Instead, focus on your Why. It's stronger than their criticism. Remember that you're pursuing your best, and you're going to find it with or without them.

Of course, you're probably thinking that what I'm telling you is obvious—that it goes without saying. Well, I'm saying it because you never know who that critic is going to be. Most will be strangers or casual acquaintances; that's to be expected. The problem is that, sometimes, your biggest opposition comes from someone close to you. It could be a sibling or parent, a child or maybe even your spouse. If you find yourself facing criticism from a person close to you, it can be that much harder, and depending on your personality, impossible to ignore. When you love and respect someone, you make yourself vulnerable to that person. They know almost all your strengths and weaknesses. That's a good thing because it enables you to have close, deep experiences with that person—experiences that fill many of the higher needs on Maslow's Hierarchy. However, that vulnerability also means the criticism will be more accurate and can hurt more.

The solution isn't an easy one either. Much of your logic and feelings will tell you it's not this simple, but the solution is simply to keep pushing forward. You can try to get that person on board with you, but there's a good chance that he or she is out of touch with his or her own Why, making it that much more difficult for them to see or accept yours. Sometimes, sitting down and sharing your Why can be enough to inspire them. But sometimes that only makes it worse. What you do to try to bring that person around is up to you; however, you can't let that person bring you down. Eventually, as you pursue your goals and reach new heights of success and self-actualization, your detractors will come around—or at least fall silent. It's hard to argue that your ideas have no merit after you've accomplished them. The good news is that those who love you will recognize the positive changes that you've made along the way and almost always come around over time. Even better, I have seen most spouses and close family members not only come around, but also find ways to participate in the experiences you are creating.

Getting Help

So there's something else you can do to help keep yourself on track. You will have detractors, but you'll also have great supporters. These are people who have actually caught sight of your vision, or like I said, it could be people who just genuinely love you and care about your success. Regardless of why they're cheering for you, be glad for it. Self-improvement is not an easy task, and you can use all the help you can get. Just because you *can* do it alone doesn't mean you *should*.

One thing you can do to readily increase your odds of success is to find some reinforcements. Some goals may be accomplished by bringing on actual reinforcements, getting other people to help you. For many personal goals, however, the change and progress is something internal or independent, and other people can't really do any of the work. That doesn't disqualify them from helping in some way though.

One of the keys to keeping yourself on track when the going gets hard is a little word that no one likes: Accountability. When you set out to accomplish something, tell everyone about it. You don't need to get in people's faces about it (that's just annoying), but don't be afraid to share the fact that you're doing something new. Tell everyone your goal because it tips the scales; it makes the price of failure that much higher—and makes you work that much harder that much longer. No one likes to be looked at as a failure, and that's exactly what will happen if you quit after telling everybody. The pressure will keep you focused.

Additionally, you really need someone you can turn to. You need a mentor of some kind even if that mentor has no experience in what you're trying to accomplish. Obviously, a mentor *with* experience is the better choice, but most successful people have walked a similar path (the one I'm explaining here). You need a person who is willing to listen to you and hear your ideas—and maybe even offer some feedback or other viewpoints. Most importantly, you need someone who can check up on you to make sure that you're staying focused and engaged.

This person can be a spouse, a friend, or a total stranger. Again, if you can find someone with experience who's willing to mentor you and keep you accountable, that's even better. You just need someone. This person can be your sounding board when times get hard and the future seems impossible. He or she can also be there to celebrate with you when you break through and make great strides.

Becoming your best self isn't an easy process. It's a long, hard road, so take what comfort you can in what you can find and move forward. Remember, your Why is the strongest force in your universe. Don't let Doubt knock you from the path and send you into Despair. Believe and have Hope, and you can make it through anything. Friends and family can help keep you accountable to yourself and your goals. You just need to start and then stay on target.

Sitting on the Seesaw

Hope, or your Core Why, is the starting point for any effective journey. If you begin your journey understanding your Why, you will start with so much more power behind you. Starting with just your What would be like starting a big semi-truck on just one cylinder. If you want to be able to pull the heavy loads and make real progress, why would you restrict yourself to a single cylinder? Why not use the whole engine available to you and maximize your power?

We've talked about how to find your Why. Now let's see what happens when we plug that into the Belief Blueprint.

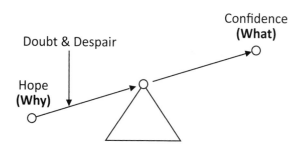

When you climb onto this seesaw, the weight of your Doubt, Despair, and negative past experiences will send you plunging down to the dirt. Looking all the way up at that goal towering high above you is intimidating. The power of your positive experiences, especially relevant ones, will help to buoy you up and carry you forward—providing fuel for you as you make the climb.

The critical element here is that you have to start with your Why if you want to rally your limbic brain. Your Hope will lift you and help you to move forward long after your neocortex would have given up, but only if you're in line with it. And here's where the importance of knowing your Why comes into play. Two people with the same What but very different Whys will have two entirely different paths to get to the same goal. Allow me to show you through a little story.

Roads Less Traveled

Back in the age of the Wild West and manifest destiny, thousands of people packed up their lives and moved west. Many of those people went to California seeking the call of riches—chasing gold. Others followed the Oregon Trail in search of land to call their own. There were also those that headed left on the map to practice their various religions and escape religious persecution. All of these people had the What of going west. They all wanted to leave the "civilized" East Coast and head out to the frontier. Their Whys were what distinguished them and their respective journeys.

My Great-Great-Grandfather, Edwin Pettit, was among the people who went west, but his Why drove him to do things a bit differently from most. Edwin's parents both died within weeks of each other when he was about 13. He and most of his siblings were appointed to a guardian in Nauvoo, Illinois, where they had been living. Edwin's older sister, who had married, was getting ready to travel west with her husband. Edwin was told that he could go with his sister, but his other siblings and his guardian opposed it. Their opposition didn't deter Edwin's Why, though, and he ran away to go west with his sister.

To Edwin's dismay, his guardian and brothers came and intercepted him on his way to his sister's camp. They dragged him home again, and he didn't get to see his sister. Still Edwin was undeterred. He wanted to find his sister and go west. His motivation was too deep to deny, so he tried again. This time, he sneaked out of the house barefoot early in the morning while his guardian slept. He didn't put his shoes on until he was out of the house. Then he and a friend ran off for the camp, walking all day until they met up with them.

Edwin couldn't actually stay in the camp at first because his guardian sent people to look for him. Instead, he slept by himself out in the prairie, shadowing the camp and traveling near the company of pioneers. When people came looking for him, the members of the camp (by instruction of the company captain) could honestly say that no one by that description was in the camp, because Edwin wasn't.

When the company crossed the Des Moines River, Edwin couldn't cross as himself or someone else leaving Nauvoo might have recognized him and turned him in. Instead, his Why was so strong that he abandoned his 13-year-old male pride and dressed up as a girl— complete with combs, fake curls, and a bonnet. He crossed the river with a group of other girls to complete his disguise, and successfully made his escape on horseback after reaching the other side.

Most people would have given up after running away and getting caught several times, but Edwin's Why was too strong. He was too determined. His What was far from unique, but his motivation drove him to take a very different path to get there. He wanted to go west to be with his sister and to start a new life with fellow believers. He wasn't after gold or land like so many who went to California, but his Why was no less strong.

Your Course

As you can see, our Why can make a huge difference in the path we choose. Edwin could have given up and stayed behind, but his Why was too strong. Because he followed it, he was successful. Ultimately, he reached the Utah territory, married, and became father to 15 children. He was also instrumental in helping people make the trip from California up to Utah, taking that journey 20 times in the course of his life. All of that happened because he followed his Why and did what was necessary to make his Hope a reality. Can you imagine what his life would have been like if he'd given up and tried to follow another person's path? If he had decided to shrug off his Why and stay in Illinois with his brothers? Can you see how getting to the What isn't the only critical element of the journey? Our Whys make our journeys uniquely perfect for us.

Your Why will provide you with the means to move forward and upward along the seesaw toward that balance point and then up a little farther until the lever tips in your favor—but only if it's *your* Why. You can't make the climb on borrowed or manufactured Whys. No matter how great the cause, you will never be able to rally the motivation unless the reason aligns with who and what you are.

This is also the way your Why can be applied to bring success in any number of different ventures. If the What can be framed in alignment with your Why, you'll find your own path to get there. You won't need to follow someone else's path. So keep that in mind the next time someone tells you you're going the wrong way to get to your destination. Perhaps you're taking a scenic route; perhaps they are. But even if that's the case, the scenery will be exactly what you need. As long as you get there in a way that enables you to still look yourself in the mirror and still sleep at night, who cares? The journey is where the real learning takes place. This is where Belief is built.

So hold on to your Hope. It'll lift you up and push you along on your journey. Also remember that there's more than one way to help you along your way. Increasing your Hope and your alignment to your Why is always a great thing to do, but it's not the only tool to help you make progress. A hot-air balloon can put more heat into the balloon to gain altitude, but it can also shed weight. Either method is equally valid.

Lightening Your Load

The stronger your Hope, the less mass you'll drop onto the seesaw, but there's another thing which can affect how much weight you bring to the seesaw when you sit down. We already talked about how it's your Doubt and past negative experience that drag you down and hold you back. In light of that, it makes sense that having more good experiences will help to propel you forward and upward. This is a logical relationship.

The question, then, is how to gain more positive experiences—or recognize more of your past ones. We're going to talk about how to gain new ones in the future over the course of the next couple sections, but there's another way I want to share with you first. It's about how to sift through your past and present in order to actually see more of the positive things that are already happening. This is something you can do to increase the strength of your Belief (making you more resistant to Doubt) while also helping you identify more of those positive moments. You can have a good attitude.

Attitude is an interpretation of your emotional state as it runs up into your neocortex. A positive attitude generally stems from positive emotions, and a negative attitude usually stems from negative emotions. However, this is one of the ways that your neocortex can exert a touch of guidance on your limbic brain. Attitude isn't entirely automatic, and I'll prove it to you.

Next time you start to feel mad, force a smile.

Now, when I say that you need to force a smile, I don't just mean make the corners of your mouth turn up. You need to actually *smile*.

Believe it or not, a true smile isn't really a factor of your mouth at all. In some cultures, the people don't really open their mouths when they smile. One thing is constant among all cultures, ethnicities, and languages though: crow's feet. Those little wrinkly lines you get at the corners of your eyes when you smile. I want you to force a smile that gives you those wrinkly lines. That act alone will send a signal to your limbic brain that you're actually happy. It's a cheap trick, but it works. The limbic brain doesn't have a capacity for deception, so it'll back off on the anger.

In this way, attitude is actually a two-way street. When you feel negative emotions welling up from within you, you will also find it easier to be negative—easier to feel Doubt creeping in. At the same time, thinking about things that make you angry—even when you're not actually angry—will trigger a measurable response from your limbic brain, accelerating your pulse and causing a physiological reaction. When you think about Doubts, it will physically affect you, depressing your body and forming a nasty feedback loop.

If you have a friend help you, you can see this effect in action. Ask that friend to hold his or her arms out straight out to the front and then push down on the person's hands. Try to remember how much resistance you feel. Next, have the person think negative thoughts and try it again. Was it easier or harder to force the arms down? Finally, just to close the loop, have that friend think about happy, positive things and push again. Logically, the third time around should have your friend feeling weakest and resisting least, right? His or her arms should already be tired from the first two tests. Are you surprised by the results?

Typically, if your friend is actually following instructions, you should meet some level of resistance the first time around, a severely lessened level of resistance the second time, and then at least the original resistance (if not more) the third time. Unfortunately, you already know the secret, but you can still try it in reverse by having your friend push down on your arms. It can be a very enlightening experience.

Want another proof about the power of attitude? Think of all the people you know. Do you know someone who, no matter what happens, will always see the downside? Have you ever seen something really good happen to that person? What was the reaction? Did he or she finally cheer up and think happy thoughts? Or was his/her attitude basically unchanged? Conversely, think about that person who never seems to get down. No matter what happens, he or she is always upbeat about it, right? That's not to say that bad days never happen, but they don't last long and certainly don't leave a lasting mark.

The limbic brain is a construct of instinct. It operates under a stimulus/response model—like an amoeba. When something good happens, the limbic brain perks up. When something bad happens, the limbic brain reacts accordingly. All the talks you've ever heard about proactivity don't apply here. Proactive behavior belongs to the neocortex. The limbic brain works on feelings and only acts according to how it *feels* at any given time; it doesn't plan ahead. Sadly, this power of the neocortex to manipulate the emotional response to events and goals often goes unnoticed—and unchecked. People frequently torpedo what little emotional connection they had to a goal by beating down their emotions rather than guiding and harnessing them.

Confirmation Bias

What we're talking about here is a power of the mind called confirmation bias. This is a sneaky thing, but you can put it to your own use once you understand it. The issue is that so much happens in life that there's no way for your neocortex to process it all. Your limbic brain could (and does), but that's because it processes on a much simpler level. It just needs to know what stimulus is being received and what response sets you up for the best chance of survival, so it doesn't register the level of detail your neocortex does.

As a result of this information overload, your neocortex has to pick and choose what it's going to focus on and what it's going to ignore. For an example of this, stare closely at your book. Focused? Okay, what color is the wall in the background? Did you have to peek? That information was being received by your eyes before you peeked, but your brain wasn't processing it. Some of you very clever readers focused really hard to not move your eyes from the book while still changing your focus to the wall in the background. You weren't reading anymore; you were paying attention to the wall without looking at it.

The brain just can't process everything it sees, hears, smells, feels, and tastes, not to mention all the emotional responses all those different sensory inputs elicit, especially in today's world of constant electronic stimuli. It's too much, so the brain establishes filters to determine what's important enough to actually get some real attention. As a result, most of what goes on around you goes on in the background and you remain basically oblivious to it. This is like the concept of white noise. You hear it at first but then it just fades into the background. Your brain only picks out the things that seem to provide valuable information—especially when those things break through the white noise of life.

As an example, I have a friend whose in-laws have a grandfather-type clock. This clock is set to begin chiming at 7 am and go off every 15 minutes until 11 pm. Whenever my friend goes to visit, the chime drives him nuts. Thanks to the time zone change, 7 am comes at my friend's 5 am and disturbs the final hours of his sleep. In talking to his in-laws, my friend found out that they don't even hear the clock anymore. It had been going off for so long that their brains didn't even register it.

The last time my friend went to visit—over Christmas, no less—he secretly turned off the chime. For the rest of his visit, he was never again bothered by the clock. Interestingly, his in-laws weren't bothered either. In fact, when he forgot to turn the chime back on before leaving and had to follow up to confess his action some weeks later, nobody had noticed that the chime was off—still. For almost a month, the chime was off and nobody noticed the difference. That's because their filters were already screening out the sound. In effect, the chime had been off for them for years; they'd just never thrown the switch to make it official.

If you've ever lived near a busy street, a set of railroad tracks, an airport, or if you're a parent, you know how this works. And it works for more than just sounds; it works in all aspects of life and for all of your senses. You don't really notice the weight of your clothes hanging from your body most of the time. You only notice briefly when you put things on and then briefly again when you take them off. The brain is geared for efficiency, and it's not efficient to waste time focusing on things that aren't important and don't change anyway.

Instead of processing everything, the brain picks out what seems to be most important and lets the rest drift by as white noise. Interestingly, the brain isn't an impartial judge. It will pick out things that best reinforce what's already going on in your mind. Your brain will use the bias of your emotional state to quietly confirm whatever you're currently feeling—hence the name confirmation bias. This is also a key mechanism in the mystical "law of attraction," but more on that later.

Negative Spiral

This plays a huge role with regard to how we see the world. Basically the brain works by only seeing the things it wants to see—even when evidence to the contrary is right in front of it. This holds true with how it evaluates experiences as well. It only really recognizes the things that happen in line with the way it sees the world. If you have a negative outlook on life, your brain will focus on the negative things that happen in order to justify and reinforce its perception. This negative view of things, in turn, will have an influence on your attitude and limbic brain, encouraging negative responses, Doubt, and eventually Despair.

Have you ever noticed how, when you're in a bad mood, it's so much easier to see all of the bad things happening around you? It's as though everyone is frowning. It's easy to notice other people's flaws— easier to notice your own flaws too. And bad things just seem to pile up on you. That traffic accident that made you late to work triggers the potential to take everything the wrong way. The poorly worded instruction from your boss—the one you would have rolled your eyes at before—now feels vindictive and attacking. It feels like he's mad at you for being late—something you had no control over. When you see your coworkers standing by the water cooler and talking, you seem to notice how they keep looking at you again and again. You have no way of knowing that they're discussing your recent success at that industry convention. Instead, you take it as them gossiping about you and how the boss seems to have it in for you for some reason. By lunchtime, you have a headache from all the irrational demands people keep placing on you, and the rest of the day just continues that downhill slide. By the time you get home, you hardly recognize yourself—and your family hardly recognizes you either—all starting with a car accident that you had nothing to do with.

But this happens to us all the time. Something small will happen—often something outside our control—and it will send us into a negative spiral where the confirmation bias works to confirm and justify the negative feelings we have. This is especially true when we're experiencing other risk factors like hunger, tiredness, and stress. These things affect the way the brain processes and make it much easier to see the negative side of things. This negative spiral can cripple us, ruin relationships, end careers, and completely derail our future success—if we let it. The problem is that it doesn't necessarily reset at night when you sleep. It can (especially when it was sleep deprivation in the first place) but it may not. The things you say and do one day will definitely affect the next day, and the next, and the next, and so on.

The solution, then, is to not get caught in a downward spiral of negativity like that. If you *do* get caught, you're basically just digging the dirt out from underneath you on the seesaw and piling it in your lap. Will that put you higher and closer to your goal or not? Yeah. Obvious answer.

For this reason, pessimists have a *really* hard time moving forward. I won't say that it can't happen, because some pessimists are able to make great strides forward against all odds (including the imagined ones). However, a negative attitude is a huge anchor. It's a massive hindrance to forward progress. If you find yourself suffering from a negative attitude, though, there's still Hope. You still have your Why, and just as importantly, you still have your Belief. They might be buried in mud and a bit worse for wear, but you still have the choice of what you're going to follow. Are you going to give in to your Doubt and Despair or fight for your Hope and Belief?

The key here is that two-way street of attitude. If you don't take conscious control, then your attitude is much more likely to default to whatever your current set of experiences and environmental inputs indicates. In today's world, there is so much emphasis placed on the negative that it's almost a counter-culture push to focus on the positive instead—but you can do it. If you let your limbic brain have sole say in what your attitude is going to be, you are giving up the power of evolution, the power of your neocortex to guide the limbic brain. You are basically devolving yourself back to an animal form.

The Power of Positive Thinking

If, however, you are willing to fight the negative slant of today's society, you will quickly see that the world hasn't really changed. Amazing, wonderful things happen every day all around us. The problem isn't that reality is worse than ever or anything of the sort. In fact, thanks to modern advances in pretty much everything, we can live better, healthier, longer lives than anyone in history. People have so much more opportunity at their fingertips (literally) than they've ever had. Ever. We just fall prey to a negative confirmation bias and fail to see it.

The truth is that life is great. There are still parts of the world that suffer from awful tragedies and endemic corruption and other problems, but the world as a whole is a much better place. Just think, 200 years ago, the whole world was suffering from those kinds of things. Now only pockets of it remain, and many dedicated, determined people are working on bringing justice and peace to those parts of the world too. The modern media may paint a bleak view of things in an effort to earn viewers and ratings (a tactic called sensationalism), but they aren't telling the full story of the world. Now, I'm not telling you to ignore opportunities to improve bad situations in the world. Just don't get caught up in the negativity.

Thankfully, the positive side of reality is actually much deeper and stronger, and it can provide a huge slingshot start for you on your journey toward self-actualization. Negativity breeds negativity, but positivity also reinforces itself—and your neocortex has huge influence over which mindset you adopt. By using your conscious mind to monitor and control your emotional state and how you view things, you can slowly shift your frame of thinking from a pessimistic view to a much more optimistic one. The neocortex has power to overcome certain limbic resistance through verbal affirmations.

In the children's story of the Little Engine That Could, the little engine kept repeating to itself that it *could* make it. The little engine had no way of *knowing* whether it could make it or not; it had never attempted the journey before with that kind of load. Still, the little engine was determined, and it kept thinking positively. Allowing Doubt to supplant Belief would have robbed it of the power of its

Hope—its Why—and left it struggling alone. Instead, the little engine rallied its positive emotions and thoughts and pushed forward.

It's never been a question to me about whether that little engine's wheels sometimes spun in place. For that frightening moment, it lost traction and was in serious risk of sliding backward. Maybe it even did slide back a little now and then. However, no matter how tough things got, the little engine never quit. It didn't give up. It didn't give place for Doubt to grow into Despair. It clung to the Hope of success and harnessed that Hope with Belief. It was no easy journey, but you could almost say that the little engine believed itself over that mountain and took an entire train of cars with it. You can supercharge your Hope with Optimism.

So what can you do to help develop this power of Optimism and positive thinking in your life? Let's discuss a few ways briefly. Before I do so, however, let me point out that there is an entire branch of psychology dedicated to this line of study, and you can find plenty of excellent material out there. I would highly encourage you to go look for a few sources to give you more ideas and details. What I offer here is only a primer, an introductory guide. This is the beginner's class and you'll seek out more when you're ready to graduate to the next level.

Optimism 101

First of all, remember that your neocortex has a huge say in your attitude. That say isn't unilateral or totalitarian by any means, but you have the strength and ability to choose your mindset. When you Believe you can do it, your limbic brain will come around to join you eventually. You just have to stand your ground and use confirmation bias on your behalf.

With that in mind, I'm going to give you a list of suggestions for things you can do to help rally your emotions to support you. This is far from comprehensive, but anyone should be able to find at least one thing from the list to help out. I've categorized them to help you see the proper applications. These ideas will help you to be more positive in the things you do.

Gratitude - This can be one of the most effective ways of keeping your mind and attitude positive. No one is grateful for bad news, so cultivating gratitude forces you to look for good things to be thankful for. In the absence of obvious good news, gratitude forces you to look for the silver lining in the storm cloud—the good that comes out of bad events.

• Always say please and thank you. This one seems obvious, but in today's hectic world, it often gets forgotten. Help yourself stay grateful by expressing verbal gratitude for even the smallest things. Want to take it up a notch? Add a name or title, like sir or ma'am, to the mix. Manners never hurt anyone, and you might just make someone else smile.

• Keep a gratitude journal. There are a few ways to do this, but the key is to record something daily. One way is to add a few new items to a master list of gratitude; e.g., two or three new, unique items each day without repeating things you've already recorded. Initially, this is pretty easy, but after about a month, you'll have used up the obvious answers and have to dig deeper. The other alternative is to describe a situation or event that made you grateful, and do it in detail. You want to record it in so much detail that you can actually *feel* the same situation when you go back and read it again.

• Play a gratitude scavenger hunt each day. Come up with categories of things you could be grateful for. Pick a couple of those categories each day and focus on identifying things in those categories. The next day, pick a couple other categories and repeat.

• Meditate or pray daily. If you believe in a divine power, you should take the time each day to thank that being for all the good things in your life. If that's not your thing, still take the time to meditate to yourself and review all the wonderful things in your life. You don't have to spend a long time doing this, 15 or 20 minutes broken up through the day is often enough, but you should spend at least some time. Doing this personally at least twice a day is powerful. Take it up another notch by including your spouse, children, or friends in these prayers or meditations.

Force a Positive Attitude - Attitude is so powerful; you need to keep it under your control and not let it run wild at the whims of your limbic brain. This isn't necessarily an easy thing, but it is extremely helpful to keep your attitude under conscious control.

- Smile every time you think about it. As before, this can't be a quick, corners-of-the-mouth smile. It needs to be a full-on, cheesy, wrinkling-of-the-eyes smile. A real smile like that can serve to reboot your mood and help you think positively again—especially when you feel like there's no reason to smile.
- Take a deep breath. When something goes wrong, take a moment to step back and breathe. Unless you're some kind of specialty surgeon, no decision is so critical that 10 seconds is going to ruin it. Especially in business, the timetable moves in hours, days, weeks, or more. Taking a minute to process bad news while breathing deep to keep yourself calm won't set you back, and it'll help you keep your cool so that you can make decisions with a level head.
- Exercise. Believe it or not, exercise will help you to be happier. I know that running a mile may sound like torture, and torture is a bad thing, but exercise helps release neurotransmitters in your head which stimulate feelings of wellbeing and positive mood. Next time you're angry, harness that anger by running it off. By the time you're done, you'll be too tired to be angry, and you will feel better once you recover again.

Mentoring Others - This is an awesome chance for a double whammy, and one of my personal favorites. You not only have to refine your senses to look for the good in what someone else is doing (making it easier to see the good that you, yourself, are doing too), but you also have the chance to push those moments of praise into someone else's life, potentially brightening that person's outlook and inspiring a trend of passing it on.

- Always preface criticism with something genuinely positive. If you need to reprimand someone or point out a flaw, begin by pointing out a strength or positive quality first. This will help you look for the positive things; it will also help others to stay out of a negative spiral.
- When you need to give negative feedback, give at least a 1:1 ratio of positive to negative. Really, you should be giving two or more pieces of positive news for each one bit of negative feedback, but you need to at least keep the scales even.
- Go out of your way to "catch people in the act" of doing good—and let them know you're watching for it. We live in an age when society has trained us to look over our shoulders out of fear of getting caught

for doing something wrong. When people know you're looking for the good, it'll encourage them to do more good. It'll also help you refine your confirmation bias to look for positive habits and actions.

Summary

Now, do yourself a favor and don't try to start all these things at the same time. If you are already doing one (or some), that's great. Keep up the good work and pick something else on the list to start on. You're not going to make a sweeping change in your attitude over-night. You need to start with just one and then work your way up from there.

As it turns out, Hope can be a fragile thing. If you aren't careful, you can smother it with your good intentions just as easily as you can crush it with bad ones. If you try to take on too much too soon, the task will start to feel overwhelming. That's your mind giving you a warning sign; your Doubts are building and turning into Despair. If you feel this happening, throttle back for a moment but don't stop. Never stop, even if you need to slow down for a bit.

Hope and Belief—harnessing your Core Why—will give you the strength and fortitude to power on and keep progressing. If you stop, you will be giving in to your Doubts and Despair. It's possible to start again, but it's harder to restart than it is to slow and then build again because you lose so much more momentum—which we'll talk about later.

Also remember that your attitude is like a control valve. Your atti-tude will determine the rate by which you gain altitude. If you are optimistic, you will advance much more quickly because you'll be building your Hope and Belief that much more quickly. Pessimists, on the other hand, tend to spend more time focused on (and therefore building) their Doubt and Despair.

Your attitude is yours to control—if you'll take responsibility. As you do, you'll grow your Hope and grow in alignment to it. In time, you'll become an unstoppable force for personal growth and change. All you have to do is get moving. So let's do that. We know your True Why. Now it's time to start moving.

TAKE ACTION

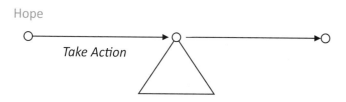

Action - [ak-shuhn]
- n. - an act that one consciously wills and that may be characterized by physical or mental ability[5]
- v.i. - to do something; exert energy or force; be employed or operative[6]

What does it mean to Take Action? As you can see from the definitions above, it means to get up and get something done. It means that you put forth a little effort—sometimes a lot of effort. The point here is movement. You know your True Why; now you need to act on it.

That Deceptive First Step

Most people would agree that the first step is the hardest one. The idea is that you're trying to overcome the physics principle of inertia to get started. You're still stationary in this Hope, and that's become the

---

[5] action. Dictionary.com.*Dictionary.com Unabridged*. Random House, Inc. http://dictionary.reference.com/browse/action (accessed: February 02, 2015).

[6] act. Dictionary.com.*Dictionary.com Unabridged*. Random House, Inc. http://dictionary.reference.com/browse/act (accessed: February 02, 2015).

status quo. Moving forward, then, violates the status quo and forces you out of your current comfort zone on some level. That's no easy task. After that, however, the thought is that you're already moving. Once you're moving, the rest will come to you over time. You've taken that first step, and now you can just keep pushing forward with whatever strength you have. Once you take the first action, you clear the way for future action.

There's a lot of sense in that line of thinking and I would almost agree on most days with respect to most journeys—but not all journeys are created equal. When you start with your Why, the power of your Hope can certainly push you along if you'll let it. You'll need to do your part to keep your Hope engaged, but it'll give you the endurance you need to forge ahead. So, when you start with your Hope in mind, you will have a much better chance of continuing to move after you overcome inertia. That's where the truth of the sentiment comes in.

However, the first step is often simply the first step. Rather than being the magical barrier to entry that needs to be overcome once and then left behind, it's just one step along the journey. For evidence of this, think back to the last New Year's resolution you didn't stick with. You may have wanted it—you may have even had your Why motivating you—yet you ultimately quit. How does that make sense? If the first step is the hardest, shouldn't it all have been an easy journey from there? Once you overcome that first hurdle, shouldn't it all be downhill?

The truth is, it doesn't get easier at this point. The first step is more like a good indicator of the difficulty of each successive step. Rather than being the hard step before the breakthrough, the first step is just that: the *first* step. If you want to get to your end destination, you'll need to take lots more steps just like it. Later on, we'll talk about the concept of Momentum and how you can build Momentum to help you carry through the hard times, but for now I need you to understand that growth requires Action. Improvement requires effort. And these amazing opportunities for self-actualization don't just require some initial influx of energy that you can then coast on forever; they require continual, sometimes continuous, inputs of no less weight than the first input.

I will grant that inertia might be the most intimidating part about starting a new journey, but I think far too many people get so caught up on beating inertia that they forget how much more there is to do in order to achieve anything lasting and worthwhile. Taking Action doesn't stop after the first action; it keeps going day in and day out forever—or until you reach your goal, whichever comes first. In fact, when it comes right down to it, I would almost say that the hardest step is the last one. That's the step where everything is on the line. Everything you've invested and built for yourself is about to either come to life or die a final death. That's a hard step, but we'll talk more about that later—including what to do if your efforts seem to explode right at the end. For now, we don't want to get too far ahead of ourselves. We're just starting out, so let's focus on what we need to know for now. Let me tell you two stories to help you see what I mean here.

Piano Practice

My parents were supportive of the things that we, as children, expressed an interest in doing. They weren't about to do the work for us, but when we expressed an interest in moving forward on a new venture, they were supportive of us. I believe that was a huge blessing and even an advantage to me as a child. However, they also set some ground rules. They didn't want us overextending ourselves or trying to get into things before we were ready, so they would sometimes tell us we had to wait before starting something new.

I experienced this as a 6-year-old child. I wanted to learn how to play the piano. For whatever reason, I thought playing the piano was this awesome thing, and I wanted to be able to do it. Problem was, I was probably still too young to start. My parents weren't opposed to me learning piano, they just didn't think I was quite old enough yet. To prove my desire in a way, I would wake everyone up in the morning by practicing scales and chords that I had figured out on my own. My first step was just convincing my parents that I was ready to start learning. That was it, right? It was easy after that, right? Not exactly. As you can see, that step wasn't easy, but the real work didn't really start until after that. Once I had permission to start early, then I had to prove myself or risk losing my chance. If I didn't make enough progress—if I wasn't diligent enough—then my parents might rethink their decision and tell me to wait until I was older after all.

So I kept up my practice regime, which you should know was easy because I loved it. I kept focusing on learning those rudimentary skills and pushing myself to get better and faster. If I found a song I wanted, I would either learn to play it or learn to alter it so that I could play it (my hands were simply too small back then to play some songs without modification). But then, after I learned those first scales and simple songs, I was done, right? I knew everything I needed to know to be a good piano player, right? Not exactly. I knew what I'd learned, and those things were becoming easy to me. However, there's more to playing piano than knowing scales and having a few simple songs memorized. I wanted to be able to pick up, read, and play anything. I now had the fundamentals to manage that, but I wasn't really skilled enough. I had to continue pushing forward and working hard even though, by all appearances, I was turning into a child prodigy of sorts.

Thanks to all that effort and energy as a child, I'm to a point today that I can pretty much play anything you put in front of me. If I can't play it "out of the box," I know enough theory that I can alter the piece so that I can play it. Additionally, as I went through this process of learning and practicing, my parents saw an opportunity to help me learn discipline too. For most kids, when they misbehave, their parents will ban them from activities like TV or video games or playing with friends. For me, I rarely got grounded from friends or told I couldn't watch TV or anything else. Those things didn't matter as much to me. Instead, my parents would forbid me from touching the piano. I didn't get sent to my room often; I got grounded from the piano—and it was awful.

After being so engaged in piano, however, do you think my journey is over? No. Some goals in life are goals that you reach and then you're done. Piano, however, is kind of like fitness. Once you reach a level of aptitude and ability, you have to continue to work at it forever in order to maintain your ability. If you want to continue to improve, you have to keep working a little harder each time you practice.

So, for me, playing the piano has been an amazing, wonderful journey. My life wouldn't be even close to the same without all the struggle and victory of what piano brought to my life. It's gotten a lot easier for me over the years thanks to Momentum (which, again, we'll talk about later), but it still takes just as much effort and time as ever if I want to improve my skill.

Ballet Training

The second story about first steps and long journeys is about my wife. To preface it, let me just say that I love my wife very much. She is an inspiration to me, and you're about to see just one of the many reasons why. In a lot of ways, she is the perfect example of how The Belief Blueprint works. Now for the story.

Around the age of 12, my wife decided she wanted to learn ballet. She started lessons and discovered she loved dancing. She practiced a lot, just like I practiced piano. While I was playing for and singing in choirs, she was joining dance companies and performing. I was training my hands, and she was training her feet!

By the time she reached college, she was good enough to make one of the ballet companies at the university. Now, I'm not glossing over her childhood in an effort to make any of what she'd done to this point seem somehow easy. Any of you who have ever danced will know that ballet is anything but easy. Any of you who have ever even pretended to dance ballet (admit it, you've tried) will have at least a vague understanding of the strength, stamina, and muscle control required. I'm glossing over the childhood stuff because it mirrors my own childhood experience closely enough that we've already covered those principles.

My wife had to put in increasing effort and time just like I did, but when she was on the ballet company, something happened that changed her ballet career forever. She developed acute Achilles tendinitis. Now, to my knowledge, there is no form of ballet out there which doesn't require major use of your Achilles tendons. Traditional ballet requires you to not only be on your feet but to be on your toes—back and forth, up and down—and often in ways that aren't perhaps physiologically ideal.

When this happened, my wife was faced with basically two choices: quit dancing altogether or keep going through the intense, agonizing pain. She took Action and pushed ahead. Her choice involved hours of physical therapy. Daily. Weekly. She would go and work out and rehearse and practice and then go and get physical therapy to counteract some of the pain and inflammation. I can still remember going to see her after her practices sometimes. Her feet and ankles would be in an ice bath or getting a deep-tissue massage. She was in pain all the time, but she couldn't give up ballet; she loved it too much. Her Why was too strong, and still calls to her today.

This is an example of someone whose journey certainly didn't get easier after the first step. Like with most opportunities for self-improvement, my wife's ballet took ever increasing amounts of effort and focus. Where her experience differs from many is that her incline turned sharply up when she got really serious about her skill. Instead of taking incremental additions of effort and patience, it took monumental additions. She couldn't even get by with putting in the same amount of effort each day, she had to put in more each day—just to compensate for the damage she had incurred the day before.

Ultimately, she did stop dancing, but not until she'd achieved her goals. In fact, to say she quit is something of a misrepresentation. In reality, she did what she'd wanted to do and then moved on to a new chapter of life. She actually spread her classes out to give herself an extra year of eligibility as a full-time student just so that she could dance more—even with the tendinitis. She still dances, but she isn't as intense about it as she once was. Thankfully, the tendinitis has also gone away with time and reduced physical stress. Most importantly, no matter how hard the trial was for her, it didn't define her story. She still looks back and remembers the challenges, but what she really thinks about are the performances she was part of and the lifelong friends she made. She looks back at the Actions she took and the success she had, not the hard times along the way.

Next Steps

Just imagine though. Imagine that every step you take causes you sharp, physical pain—while dancing, yes, but also while simply walking around. How's that for an obstacle to your Action? I wouldn't want to move. I think back to times when I've started a new workout program and how sore I end up. Men can kind of be babies about pain sometimes. I hardly want to move when I'm sore like that. These kinds of things show us just how strong our Hope is, though. How much Hope and Belief my wife must have been carrying inside her to push forward when every step caused pain? You have that same strength inside you when it comes to your Hope.

That's your Core Why, and it will help you push forward and Take Action even when each step can seem to be harder than the last one. So free yourself of the misunderstanding that the first step is the hardest one. First steps aren't easy, but they aren't the end either. Subsequent steps are often harder. In fact, the next step you take is likely to be the hardest one yet.

I don't say this with an intent to discourage you, but to explain in detail what it means to grow your belief. Remember, I never quit practicing my piano no matter how tedious or difficult it sometimes was. Even better, think of how my wife would push forward in spite of the intense, physical pain. Your Core Why is plenty strong enough to carry you through the hardship required to reach any worthy goal—so long as you continue to Take Action and move forward. You may have to slow down from time to time, but you should never stop.

The reason I point out that the first step is often one of the easier steps is because I see a trend in people where they set themselves up for failure on the first step. This idea that the first step will be the hardest tends to blind people to the reality of the second step. I see people all the time who psyche themselves up to take that first pivotal step and then crash when they see the next one. I'm a realist, and I want you to have a realistic view of the journey. Your Hope is strong enough to carry you through, but you have to be able to keep your neocortex engaged. You can't let Doubt destroy your Belief, and thinking that getting started is the hardest part is a quick way to open yourself to Doubt over time.

Your Dream House

So be careful about how much time you spend trying to pump yourself up for that first step. You're preparing for a marathon, not a sprint. You need to be focusing on your endurance, not your burst strength. And don't try to take in the whole journey at once either. Start out walking if you have to. Anything worth doing is worth doing right, and doing things right takes time and consistent effort—it takes Action.

The world of self-actualization is full of long journeys and high elevations. The sheer scope and size of some efforts makes them almost impossible to look at outside the conceptual level. This is where the midbrain comes in handy. The midbrain enables us to grasp onto huge, dreamy, abstract goals and intentions even though we can't possibly comprehend all the parts.

To demonstrate this, let's think about your dream house. How many rooms does it have? How many of those are bedrooms? Do you have just enough for your family or do you have a few extra for things like a home office, gym, or guest rooms? What color are the appliances? Do the ones in the kitchen match the ones in the laundry room? How many floors does it have? Are you on a single level? Multiple levels? Does it have a basement? What kinds of rooms will you put in the basement?

Spend a few minutes thinking about all the neat features of your dream house. Try your best to imagine everything in such detail that it feels like you're walking through that house. What color is the paint in the hall? How many windows do you have in the living room? Are you going to have carpet or hardwood? Or a combination? Will you tile the bathrooms or do some kind of linoleum? Are you going to do showers, tubs, or combos? Does that vary depending on the bathroom? How many bathrooms will you have? Where will they be located?

Is your brain starting to burst yet? If it is, that's actually a good thing. I'm actually *trying* to get you to envision so many details that your neocortex overloads. By now, you have probably forgotten the first few questions I asked. That's okay. That's intentional. I want you to start to realize how huge of a task it is to build a house.

Now let's go even deeper. How many nails will it take to build that house? How many 2x4s? How much plywood and sheetrock? How many man-hours of labor? How many yards of concrete? How many yards of wiring? Or do you need miles? What about plumbing? These questions are a bit more difficult, aren't they? We're starting to go beneath the surface to the smaller pieces of the whole, and that requires even more thought and planning.

In fact, once you've picked a site for your dream home, what do you think is the very first step to building it? Do you just start digging? Do you clear the trees and shrubbery first? Maybe you should go and get your permits before you do anything else, right? I'll give you a hint. Even before the permitting process, before you clear the land, before you dig out the ground for the foundation, you need to draw up some plans. In connection with that, you probably need to run some surveys of the land and surrounding areas. A contractor could give you even more specifics on what you need to do, but we're specific enough for our purposes at this point. Ready? Go do it.

The Vision

Are you starting to feel a bit overwhelmed yet? Good. You should be. That was my intention. Goals for improving yourself are a lot like this dream house of yours. On the surface, it might not look like there's a whole lot to them. They are beautiful and emotionally stirring and you feel deep longing for the day when that thing is yours. However, there's a lot of work—a lot of Action—that goes into getting that far.

It's important to have that vision of the finished product, but it's also important to recognize that you're not going to go from unde-veloped lot to dream house overnight. One of the big reasons people fail at the big goals in life is because they're content to simply dream; sometimes it's because they get so overwhelmed by the enormity of the effort that they give up instead of moving forward.

The vision of your ultimate destination, your What, is important because it will rally your Hope, but you can't spend all your time rallying without ever getting a move on. You need to move forward a bit at a time. You need to get started on building the dream house in some way. How you start isn't so important. You can go out and buy a box of nails or a couple 2x4s. You can go down to the county office and start working on your permits. You can start the land surveys. As long as you start somewhere at the beginning and then keep moving forward, the specific step isn't quite as important. Just don't get ahead of yourself and start putting the roof on before you have the walls up. You can't even pour the foundation until you've dug the hole for it.

Some things have to go in order—you have to walk before you can run—but some things don't. The most important thing is to continue to Take Action at whatever level you're on. If you stop taking action, you'll start to backslide on the seesaw. Sometimes, that means you have to take very small steps in order to prevent yourself from losing ground. That's okay too. Baby steps are a great way to get going.

Learning to Walk

Thinking about babies, have you ever watched a baby learn to walk? It's a fascinating study in setting goals, starting small, and trying again after each failure. When babies first come out, they can't really do anything but lie there and cry. Over time, they wiggle and move in an effort to build strength—but why? Every need is taken care of. What is the incentive to do anything more?

That's instinct in the limbic brain driving the baby to mimic what it sees. Mom and Dad are moving around on two legs, and the baby imprints that and tries to mimic it. In time, the infant will develop enough strength to start rolling over on its own. Then it will start trying to push up off the ground. Every action the baby takes is designed to increase strength and enable that infant to copy what it sees. Its Why is driving it to become like the people it sees all around.

Eventually, with no help or training, that baby will teach itself to get up on all four limbs and then start moving around that way. But the baby doesn't see its parents crawling around all the time, so that instinct to improve keeps driving it on. Pretty soon, that baby is pulling itself up on the furniture, on its parents' legs, on the family dog, on the wall, or on anything else it can find. The baby will fall over and over again, but even this is actually a learning step. The baby needs to learn how to fall properly so it doesn't spill over and bonk its head on the floor or coffee table every time it goes down.

After enough practice in pulling up and falling, the baby won't be satisfied with just pulling up on things. It'll pull itself up on the end table but then want to go over to the couch to see Grandma. That baby is then faced with a choice. It can drop to the ground, crawl over, and pull itself back up, or it can try to do what its parents have been demonstrating for months. The baby will take that first, tentative step—and fall on its face.

Time to call it quits, right? The poor toddler took Action and failed, so it's time to find something else to go after, right? No. The Why inside that baby is too strong. It'll crawl to Grandma that time and be trying to take steps again before the hour is through. Pretty soon, that baby will be pulling itself up in the middle of the floor with no help and then walking all over the place. Then running, dancing, swimming, somersaulting, and more. We learn two critical lessons here. The first relates to step size. The second is about failure.

Baby Steps

When that baby is first learning to walk, how big are those steps? Pretty tiny and halting, right? It takes the smallest possible steps because it is so focused on balance. As the toddler grows, balance will become more and more instinctive and second nature, and the steps will get bigger and bigger until that child can run, jump, and do any number of other activities.

The key here is to remember that those initial steps are tiny. Just like when you go to start building a dream home, you have to think and dream big but then break it down and start small. The baby doesn't start by jumping away from the end table any more than you can start with the roof when building a house. The journey of self-improvement starts the same way. You have to start small and start basic.

People begin to lose their Hope when they try to take on more than they can handle at any one time. They have huge goals and their Whys are so strong that they jump in with both feet—and quickly start drowning. This is another testament to the strength of the limbic brain and Hope, but it can quickly prove self-defeating when left unchecked. Instead of diving in headfirst and trying to sprint to the finish, people need to realize that worthy endeavors take effort over time. You can't cram for success; it doesn't work.

Success comes by understanding that the journey to a destination doesn't follow the shortest line between points A and B. In the real world, success is the journey between points A and Z—passing through each letter in sequence along the way. People get tripped up when they try to go from A to Z in one step—or even from A to C. You have to pace yourself and take things in manageable steps, one step at a time.

The 10 Percent Rule

Long ago, I heard about a technique that can help with bringing your focus down from the big picture to the next baby step. The concept is to limit your scope to the things that you can work on immediately. When you're learning to walk, you don't benefit by thinking about how complicated it will be to jump. When you're building a house, you don't worry about getting the lighting in the kitchen just right when you're still pouring the foundation and framing in the walls.

People do this all the time though. They get so caught up in all the details down the road that they exhaust themselves and lose touch with their Hope. They overburden their Why with problems that don't even exist yet. After all, who doesn't like to play the "What If" game?

I'm going to ask you to do your best to stop. The "What If" game will sink your Hope and expose you to Doubts. Unfortunately, our nature is that the "What If" game never asks questions like "What if someone helped me?" or "What if the stars aligned in my favor?" Instead, we just look for all the ways things could go wrong. We do this as a defensive measure to steel ourselves against the pain of failure, but it also frequently turns into a sort of self-fulfilling prophecy. When we spend all our time figuring out how to not fail—instead of planning for how to succeed—we usually end up failing. Sadly, we then use that failure as justification for continuing to play the "What If" game in the future. We tell ourselves that we just save ourselves from a world of hurt and that we should continue to protect ourselves the same way in the future.

There's a way out of this though. The problem stems from the way most people switch back and forth between the big picture and the immediate next step. The immediate next step often feels so small and insignificant that we would much prefer to just focus on the big picture. Keeping our focus there leaves too much uncertainty between us and the end goal, leaving plenty of room for questions and Doubts to creep in.

Instead of switching from big picture to immediate view and back again, we need some sort of intermediate level. There is a helpful solution I've heard explained in many different ways by many different successful people who have worked through complex projects or situations. For our purposes here, we'll call it the Ten Percent Rule. Using the 10 Percent Rule means focusing on only the next 10 percent of your journey. Instead of thinking about the whole project, you just think about the next cluster of related items. This focuses your view enough so that your mind can wrap around your What yet still retain a level of detail sufficient to avoid the "What If" game. You can see the immediate next step and several steps beyond toward some larger, more definable goal without having to try to grasp the entire process in your head at one time. We'll talk more about how to do this in just a bit.

Coping with Failure

First, we need to go back to the second lesson we learn from watching a baby learn to walk. This lesson relates to how we handle failure along the way. Taking Action is a key to success. You can't ever get anywhere or become something better than you already are if you don't ever Take Action. Unfortunately, the moment you do Take Action, you open yourself to setbacks—sometimes called failures.

True failure can only happen when you give up. Suffering from setbacks or speed bumps along the way happens to everyone. That's part of the process of heading for triumph. In a way, you can think of these things as part of the currency of buying success. You have to put in so much effort—and experience so much frustration—before you'll finally reach your destination. Giving up, however, is like closing the account. You're walking away from an unfinished project.

What most of us call failure really isn't. What we actually experience is difficulty, unanticipated consequence, hardship, setback, side-effect, mistake, etc. That said, we often experience true failure too, but that's always related to our personal choices to give up—though giving up isn't always failure (more on that later).

This is where we think back to that baby and its quest for mobility. The baby doesn't give up on walking. No matter how many times it experiences setbacks—or even physical pain—it will continue to get up and try again. Babies know, instinctively, that they can learn from each setback. They learn one more way to not walk—and then they don't try to walk that way again. Eventually, they'll be able to take a few steps without falling. Then they'll get to the point that they can walk for short distances, then long distances. Each milestone comes with plenty of setbacks and mistakes, but each milestone comes after Taking Action in the face of those difficulties.

Remember that going from where you are to where you want to be isn't a simple journey from point A to point B; it's an A to Z journey with plenty of steps in between. You're going to experience setbacks and problems as you go through that process. On the journey from A to B to C and so on, sometimes you'll find that what you *thought* was C really isn't. You'll go from B to C only to realize that C is really somewhere else. At that point, you can give up and quit, never achieving your goal, or you can be like the baby. You can pick yourself up, backtrack to point B, and start out in the new direction.

Can you imagine what would happen if a baby quit after that first fall? After the second fall? Most of us were still tripping over our own feet for years after we "learned" to walk. Some of us still trip over our own feet even decades after we should have been experts! If you'd quit the first time you put your foot down the wrong way, you'd never have gotten anywhere.

Revisiting Doubt

So why do we quit? Because it's painful to be wrong. Taking Action often requires stepping into the darkness. You Believe you know what to do to take you closer to your goal. You Hope you know what to do, so you take a step—and fall on your face. That can be humiliating when seen in public, but it can be painful enough even when nobody else knows. Worse still, it can make you doubt your ability to achieve your goal at all.

Feeling like you're flailing around without making any progress can leave you feeling beaten and broken. When you finally see some progress, it can be a revitalizing feeling, but all the bumps and bruises along the way can also leave you feeling weak and broken. For many people, having those little failures along the way can lead to questions—to Doubts. When things don't go according to plan, they are left wondering why not. Worse still, they are often left wondering whether the whole endeavor was flawed to begin with.

Wondering why your immediate plan didn't work can actually be very instructive. This kind of introspection can lead to important revelations regarding your motivations (your What and Why). It also leads to critical learning and information about what to change on your next attempt. This self-discovery and contemplation turns the experience from error to enlightenment and enables you to course correct and get back on track. It becomes one of those thousands of little falls the baby makes on the path to mobility.

When the little hiccups along the way make us question the overall goal, however, we run into serious problems. These kinds of feelings can quickly bury us with Doubt, crushing our Hope and Belief. Sadly, human nature is kind of losing its edge. Instinct is being trained away into complacency. Instead of striving to become more and more every day, many people are content with mediocrity. The majority of societies on the planet ensure in some way that basic human needs are being met. The incentive to perform is lowered. This means that people today are much more likely to throw up their hands and walk away at the first sign of difficulty. You can see this in the number of failed business ventures, failed marriages, and college dropout rates, among other places.

People seem to be less and less willing to Take Action in the face of difficulty—especially when they've already had some mistakes or hit some speed bumps along the way. So many people are giving in to their Doubts and fears instead of remembering that baby steps can move them forward. Then, when they see someone who isn't afraid to fail, they may even get defensive and bitter about it.

Overnight Success

One of the places we see this is when someone seems to suddenly burst onto the stage of success. It's like they were just sleeping their way along only to explode into the limelight. Often, we're tempted to look at these people and ascribe their sudden victory to luck or divine intervention. Do you know what luck really is? Skill and timing. Also, I won't argue that divine intervention doesn't exist, but I will point out that God tends to help those who help themselves. He doesn't generally reach out and elevate people who are standing still.

This attempt to explain away the sudden trappings of another person's success stems from the knowledge that we aren't making maximum use of our own efforts. This deficit comes from shying away from being our best—from letting our Doubts get the better of us. No one likes to be reminded of failure, and one of the easiest ways to get a reminder is to see someone else be successful in a goal where you failed—or one you would like to achieve but have never tried.

Can I tell you a secret? There's no such thing as an overnight success. There's only such a thing as an overnight blossoming of someone's success. You could argue that social media has changed all this, but it really hasn't. It may have shortened the curve and lowered some barriers to entry for some markets and goals, but the process is still there. No one becomes a super star singer, for example, without having put in the time to practice. You can see that perfectly in the experiences of shows like American Idol. Some of the people who show up aren't participating in reality. They have no chance because they've put in no effort. The winners, however, never talk about how they decided to enter on a whim and had never sung a day in their lives. No. They talk about how many years they'd been hoping and praying for the chance to make it big—I can guarantee you that Hope and prayer weren't the only things going on. They were also practicing, developing skills. They were Taking Action.

That's the secret behind the apparent overnight successes. They aren't successful at something because they woke up one morning, wrote a nice email and suddenly made it big. They have been taking baby steps for years in the background. While other people were sitting around dreaming, they were singing in their bedroom mirrors. When others were staring at the kid with the lemonade stand across the street, these successes *were* the kid with the lemonade stand across the street. And they were probably gouging their customers while still selling at a loss—all without even knowing it. Those steps, however, led to more steps and put those people in a place to be ready when the opportunity finally arrived.

In fact, I would actually say that they didn't just prepare for their opportunity to shine; they *made* their opportunity to shine. It's not like someone came to their door and said, "You seem well prepared for this role." Instead, these people were preparing while simultaneously putting themselves in positions where they could connect with opportunity. They were Taking the Action of going to the right places. They were putting themselves in the right place and then preparing themselves for the right time. It wasn't until that "right time" that anyone noticed them or how much effort they'd put in. Once people did notice them, many of those same people conveniently ignored all the effort and time spent preparing.

And you don't need to sprint ahead. Steady pacing is just fine. Remember the fable about the Tortoise and the Hare? The Hare never makes it to the finish line in that story because he can't stay focused. He's so fast and has so much potential but he lets himself get distracted from the task at hand. The Tortoise, on the other hand, plods forward at a nice, measurable pace. Where the Hare is always looking for the next big thing, the Tortoise is focused on Taking Actions that move him forward.

You can't build a house overnight. You can't cram a house either. You have to start Taking Action and then move forward at a logical, steady pace. It takes time for concrete to set before you can build on the foundation. It takes time for inspectors to come out and clear the various stages of construction. It takes time to run the wiring and plumbing before you can put the walls up. If you try to leave everything until the last minute, you'll fail. If you try to do it all overnight, you'll fail. Even doing it too quickly can result in flaws that may prove detrimental over time.

Goal Setting Crash Course

When you set your goals, you need to recognize that they will take time—and then you need to be willing to put in that time starting right away. Writing this book, for instance, couldn't be done overnight. It takes time to key in all the letters to make words to make sentences—not to mention the mental stress of presenting all the material in a way that makes sense and putting it all in the right order. Goals are the same way. They require effort *over time*. You can't expect to put in all the effort one day and have the result come trickling back to you after that—you wouldn't like the kind of result that trickled back in that instance.

We have a fairly serious problem in our society in which we think that you can just muscle through a goal with a concerted, serious effort over a short period of time. Tell me, when was the last time you tried to force a relationship with someone? A parent, spouse, child, or friend? Did it work? I didn't think so. Where does this notion that we can just power through things come from? Would you believe me if I said it probably came from the movies?

Think about it. Where in *real* life have you ever seen a person get up one day, decide to make a sweeping improvement in his or her life, and enjoy raging success by dinner? It doesn't happen in that kind of time frame in real life, does it? It happens all the time in TV and movies though, doesn't it? Even video games require you to put in time and effort to get stronger. In fact, it's that virtual fiction of accomplishment that keeps people going back for more.

But where's the entertainment in watching someone slave away for hours, days, weeks, or years to get better? How boring. Instead, we see the hero (or heroine) at the beginning looking just as clumsy, incapable, and awkward as we usually feel. Then, after a few minutes of training snippets, that person is suddenly primed to save the world—so that we can get to the good part and the happy ending. This impossibly rapid transformation is usually attributed to secret government training programs or intense strength of will. Either attribution is equally ridiculous. As we've discussed, your willpower resides in your neocortex. Where does the real power to push for change and achievement come from? A hint—not your neocortex. Your Why is your Hope and it's in your limbic brain.

So let's talk about goals in real terms. Let's talk about how you realistically set and attain those dreamy, impossible goals you've always had but have always been too scared to tackle. This isn't really a goal-setting book, but I can't claim to have taught you about how to reach for self-actualization if I don't at least cover goals for a few pages. So let's talk about how the 10 Percent Rule works in practice.

Visualization

As we begin, let me just point out that there are tons of different goal-setting methods out there. I'm going to talk about a couple general rules that make the most sense to me and have the most effect in the lives of people I've worked with, but you are welcome to use whatever specific method or technique you want. Conveniently, these general theories of responsibility apply to all the other universal laws of goal setting, so everyone has something to gain here even if you go on to use a different, more-specific method to set your personal goals.

Let me briefly lay out the entire process for you, and then we'll dive into the individual steps. First, you decide where you want to go; you pick your What. Then you rally your Why behind your What. Now you have trajectory! Third, you break down the goal into segments you can hold in your mind. Fourth, you further break those segments into actionable A-to-B-to-C steps. Fifth, you get up and Take Action.

Step One: Pick Your What

The first step to any goal is to decide What you're doing. Where are you going? We kind of talked about that before. Now we're going to get specific. You know your Core Why—what drives you—now you need to decide where it's going to take you. Indulge me with this next example so that you can understand what I mean.

Ever since they were produced in 1992, I've had a fascination with Dodge Vipers. For whatever reason, the curves of that car speak to me. I've always wanted one—in spite of the price tag. That car is an inspiration to me of sorts. When I was younger, I wanted it just because it was a super-fast, exotic-looking sports car. I hadn't really connected with my Why yet, so I was really just focused on the Whats in life, and it seemed like life should include a car that went fast enough to leave sanity behind.

To this day, I retain that eye for Dodge Vipers. I have a Vision Board (which we'll talk more about in a moment) which still has a picture of a Dodge Viper today (they're actually SRT Vipers now; Dodge sort of spun off the division, but I digress). You know what's crazy about it though? I'm at a point in life where I could get a Viper, but I don't have one. I'm not sure if I'll ever buy one. I still think they're attractive, amazing vehicles, but I've learned more about my Why.

Step Two: Align to Your Why

My Why includes being financially independent. I want to have the resources to go out and get anything I want—but that doesn't mean I have to go out and actually buy stuff. I like the car I drive, at the moment it's a paid off Toyota Corolla. I don't need the Viper for any legitimate reason. I don't street race (or track race, for that matter). I'm not auditioning to be a racecar driver. I'm not trying to impress anyone with the flashy-ness of my car. The reason that Viper has stayed on my Vision Board is because it doesn't even represent the car to me anymore. It represents that concept of financial independence to me. If I can afford to buy a Viper, then I'm financially independent. The image of the car isn't about the car anymore. It's about my Why. Ironically, it's probably more about my family and peace of mind than any kind of midlife crisis.

So, in this case, my Why is financial stability and independence. I want to know that I can afford to support my family no matter what happens. That's my Why. That's an emotional, deep, instinctual drive for me. I represent that with the image of a Dodge Viper—a What—that I can work toward. Even if I never buy the car, having that image in my head triggers the emotions of my Why and helps me push forward on the days when I want to quit. That image helps me Take Action when I think I'm too tired to go on. That's the power of visualization.

A Vision Board helps you to harness this power by keeping your Whats and Whys in front of you where they can influence you and motivate you. Sometimes, when we start out on a goal, we can get so buried in minutia that we start to forget why we're even doing it. Maybe you've even felt that way about your job. "Why do I even bother doing this?" A Vision Board answers that question. It reminds you Why you got started.

Vision Boards come in all shapes, sizes, and mediums. It can be a text document on your computer, a corkboard on the wall of your cubicle, a mosaic you paint in your basement, or a collage you keep above the kitchen sink. The medium doesn't matter as long as it has meaning to you. The location doesn't really matter either as long as you have quick, easy access to it in the moments when you are most likely to struggle. For example, if your low points tend to come in the middle of the day while you're at work, you should probably keep your Vision Board (or at least a current copy) at work. On the other hand, it doesn't do you much good to keep it at work if your hardest times come on the weekend or in the evenings when you're at home. Plan ahead and keep it where you need it. If necessary, keep a picture of it on your phone so you have it at all times. Just remember to update the picture when you update your Vision Board.

It's okay to update your Vision Board over time. In fact, it's almost required. As you reach targets on your board, take them down and replace them with something else—or just re-imagine them like I did with my Viper. If your target is a new job (or a new TV) you'll need to come up with a new goal once you land the job (or buy the TV). Each time you make a new goal, you should be updating your Vision Board in order to remind you how the What connects to your Why and keep you motivated to Take Action.

Incremental Progress

The first two steps of this goal-setting method really revolve around visualization. If you aren't motivated to do something, you won't do it no matter how well planned it is. If your heart isn't in something, it'll show, and you might as well stay home and spend some time in thought. It's better to take that extra time to really get yourself fully engaged before starting out. If you try to lead off too early, you're more likely to experience Doubt when you face difficulty.

So make sure you don't skip the first two steps—or even try to rush through them too quickly. Spend the time you need to in order to get yourself fully on board. Once you're fully in the game, it's time to create your plan of attack. The expression "fools rush in" applies here. I understand the concern that planning out your approach to a goal can take precious time. I even understand that some people worry about losing their motivation while they're in the planning phase. To those people, let me say this: If you lose your motivation while you're steeped in thinking about your goal, you probably have the wrong goal. Planning out your goal should excite you because you should start to see how it can all come together and come true. With that in mind, let's go on to the next steps. These steps are focused more on the concept of baby steps and how to get you there.

Step Three: Break It Down

Once you have your goal set and you're fired up from Visualizing, you're ready to get out there and attack that goal, right? Sure, but let's plan out that attack. Focus on the How. Can you imagine what would happen to a football team if they got themselves all hyped up by visualizing the win only to run out on the field without calling a play? How would the players know what to do? How would they know where to go, who to block, or even who was supposed to make the play? Your receivers might dogleg the wrong direction right when the quarterback throws the ball. The team would look like a bunch of kids with no skill—no leadership.

Goal setting is personal leadership in its purest form. It's taking control of yourself and your course and putting them under your conscious direction and control. You're planning experiences that build your belief. Getting yourself pumped up and ready to Take Action is the critical first phase, but you need to know what Action to take or you'll end up running around and wasting excessive amounts of effort without achieving any kind of tangible results. You want to talk about a quick way to cultivate Doubt and confusion leading to Despair? I can't think of a more effective way to torpedo yourself.

To figure out what Action to take, you need to start by taking your main goal and breaking it down into logical parts. Before I explain further, I issue a caution to the perfectionists: don't overthink this part and don't get mired down in the details. This process should go fairly quickly and whatever you conclude today should remain fluid as it will definitely evolve as you go. In fact, as I mentioned previously, it will probably look nothing like what you have envisioned. That's not the point of thinking through your goals. The plan you come up with is simply a way to start moving right away. It's extremely helpful to think through every possibility so you're prepared for what may come. Let's get back to how to break it down.

If you're trying to get a new job, for instance, you might break that down by the prerequisite skills you need to obtain in order to fully qualify. You can look at the job description and pull out the critical skills and call each of those things a subset. It's okay if these things are still a bit general at this point. We'll fix that in Step Four. For now, you just need to break the goal down into phases that are more manageable.

If you have a really big, dreamy goal and the first round of breakdown still leaves you with subgoals too big to really wrap your head around, pick the first one and break it down further. Again, these little subgoals can be a little vague still, but you should be able to see how they are pointing you in the right direction even if they aren't giving you all the directions. Once you complete that first set of sub-subgoals, return to this step and break down the next subgoal the same way. You don't necessarily want to break all of the subgoals down just yet because your understanding of how to break them down will evolve as you go through and do the pieces of the first subgoal. Change is the only constant.

Let me walk you through a physical example of this process so you can see the concepts in action. In terms of a car, you can think of the overall goal as the finished car. Subgoals might be the various systems in or sections of the car, like chassis, engine compartment, drive train, seating, HVAC, etc. If those subgoals are still too big to really think about, you could then further break those down by picking one and subdividing again. We'll start with the chassis. You might break it down into suspension, frame, etc.

Now you're getting into subsets small enough that you can actually deal with the entire thing in your mind at one time. There are still plenty of individual pieces involved in the suspension of your car, but you can pull off the wheel and see almost all of them right in front of you. It's a smaller system to try to hold in your mind at once.

The key here is to make sure that you end up with pieces that are small enough for you to finally see the component parts—the parts that don't need to be subdivided any further. The number of levels you need to break down a goal won't be the same as someone else either, so you can't really cheat and compare notes here. Your friend might be much better or worse at conceptual thought. In that case, he or she might be comfortable with much larger pieces or might need to break things down even further. It depends on the individual.

Step Four: Make Action Items

Once you have things split into conceptual pieces that you can hold in your mind and understand, you're ready for the fourth step. In this step, you're going to pick one of those pieces and break it into the component parts. In effect, you're taking the conceptual subgoal and turning it into a checklist of all the things you need to do to accomplish that subgoal. Your intention here is to create a list of Action items— things you can go out and act on. With that in mind, none of these things should take longer than about a day at most. Realistically, it's best if you can break them down even more than that so that no step will take more than an hour or so.

Having the pieces subdivided to such a level enables you to go through and check the boxes. You don't have to stop and wonder what's next. You don't have to question whether you're doing the right thing. You've plotted the course from A to B (by planning out all the steps from A to Z in between). There may be some uncertainty left further down the line, but in what you face right now the course should be clear.

In fact, if you aren't sure about how to plot out all the steps to get to the completion of your subgoal, you might need to go back to

Step Three and break that subgoal into smaller parts. Progress is hard enough all on its own. There's no need to introduce more Doubt or chance by leaving your plan up in the air. After all, failure to plan is a plan to fail. Headaches and hardships are par for the course; you'll face setbacks along the way, but that doesn't mean you want to throw open the doors and invite problems in. It's painful and frustrating enough to deal with the issues that crop up all on their own.

So take the time to focus and build your list of steps to get to that first milestone. Remember, you don't need to plan the whole journey right now. I understand the undertaking that would be. In fact, people who do that often get so overwhelmed by the number of things they'll have to do that they give in to their Doubts and let their Hope turn to Despair. This will also put you in a mindset to accept changes to the plan as they come. Be flexible. Build the list just for the current subgoal. When you reach that waystation, pause and plan out the steps from there.

This also introduces more flexibility into your planning process, making room for growth and development along the way. Just like the baby starting out, your first Actions will likely be small and halting. As you go, however, you'll gain familiarity and Experience (which we'll talk about in the next chapter), and those things will help you to lengthen your stride.

Step Five: Take Action

Which leads up to the final step: get up and start. You have your map; you know the landmarks; you want to reach the destination; what are you still waiting for? This is when we get to that critical first step. The one that starts you on the journey. Sure, it constitutes a departure from the status quo, but who really likes the status quo anyway? If people really liked the status quo, no one would ever read this book because no one would ever want to change.

So rally your courage, your What, and your Why, and then Take Action. Take that first pivotal step toward being your best. You already know the steps out to the first basecamp, so start taking them. One at a time at whatever pace you can manage. Don't worry if you can't sprint it right out of the gate. The Tortoise beat the Hare in spite of his limited capability because he was steady. The Tortoise stayed on track and kept moving. That's the true beauty of goal setting—you'll get to your destination if you just keep going.

Walk Long Enough

In fact, we've already talked about the principle of perseverance and you may not have even realized it. In the overview at the beginning of the book, I brought up an exchange between Alice and the Cheshire Cat from *Alice's Adventures in Wonderland*. In that brief conversation, the Cat imparts several grains of pure truth to Alice. We've already talked about how you need to know where you're going or else your efforts could end up wasted when they have no direction (and we'll talk about it again later in more detail). That is commonly looked at as the lesson to be learned from this particular excerpt, and it's a good lesson, but I have another.

The second key is in the very last line of the Cheshire Cat's advice. I'll repeat the line here to refresh your memory: "*if you only walk long enough.*" If you keep taking action, you'll eventually get where you're going. There is no distance so far and no speed so slow that you can't start today and eventually reach that distant point. The longer the distance and slower the speed, the longer the journey will take, but you'll still get there if you just keep moving. You just have to walk long enough. I constantly remind myself and others that time will pass anyway. Why not be working toward something?

You can think of this a lot like trying to buy something on layaway. Maybe you've never bought anything by putting it on layaway before, so I'll explain how the process works. With layaway, you go into a store and make a purchase, but you don't fully pay for it then and you don't get to take it home. That's a key difference between layaway and credit. When you buy on credit, you get the item so long as you keep up on the payments (typically plus interest). With layaway, you don't get the item until you've paid in full (but typically without interest).

Layaway is, in effect, a store pledging that you can have a certain item once it's paid for. The store will pull your item from the shelves and store it in a back room somewhere to make sure that your individual item doesn't get sold by mistake. Even if every other copy of that item sells out, yours will still be safe and sound in the back room—as long as you keep paying for it.

This process of moving toward self-actualization, of gaining Confidence, is a lot like layaway. You know the item—the What—that you'll get at the end, and now you have to start paying the price. That payment comes in the form of Taking Action to gain Experience. We'll talk about Experience more in the next section. For now, you just need to understand that you can make large payments over a short time in order to finish paying for your item, or you can make small payments over a long time to finish paying. Either way, you'll eventually pay for your What and get to have it—and the Confidence you gain will be yours forever.

Focus Forward

Where people most often run into problems with this is when they start comparing themselves to others. It's pretty easy—especially on a bad day—to look around and see all the other people who seem to be doing so much better than you are. What you don't see in that snapshot of a moment is how much effort that other person has put in for however long he or she has been putting in that effort.

Think of it like a freeway. When you start driving on the freeway, there will be cars that pass you (unless you have a lead foot) and cars you pass. You can see, in that moment, whether you are traveling more quickly or more slowly than the other car, but you have no idea of that other driver's destination. More importantly, you have no idea which exit that person used to get on the highway. For all you know, that little car that just shot by got on two exits after you and has no intention of traveling as far. On the other hand, maybe that person's been driving cross-country for days and has hundreds of miles still to go before arriving.

The point is, you have no idea what the people around you are going through. You have no idea how much time and effort they are putting in to get where they are. When someone seems to have a Midas touch, you can rest assured that the person isn't getting much sleep and probably has almost no idea what the latest, greatest TV shows are. There are a lot of hours in a day, and you can get a lot of work done if you buckle down and do it. The more you do today, the further along you'll be tomorrow. Keep that up long enough and you'll achieve your goal.

Spend all your time looking around at others and you won't be moving forward. If you're moving at all, you'll be weaving side to side like you're texting at the wheel. You don't know how much effort they've already put in, but telling yourself that they have it easy is a surefire way to stir up your own Doubts. Thing is, that whole perception is skewed and untrue. As it turns out, we really all have the same chance at things, we just don't see it that way.

Level Playing Field

We don't see it that way because of our individual pasts. We all come into this world as defenseless, helpless, screaming babies. There are plenty of things that can happen after that point which can appear to tip the scales in a person's favor (or turn the tables against you), but the truth is that there aren't really any cosmic Actions without equal and opposite reActions. People born with a silver spoon in their mouths, for instance, often struggle to ever develop self-motivation. They have "everything" already, so why learn to work? On the other hand, people born with nothing need to learn to work like crazy just to stay alive, but they have the challenge of overcoming social and personal stigma—the belief that they aren't worthwhile.

You can see how this works with the Belief Blueprint. Before you get on it, the path to Confidence, success, and self-actualization is nice and level.

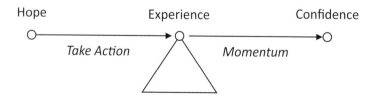

Once you hop on, however, the model tips under the weight of all your Doubt and emotional baggage from all your concerns and fears, and they weigh down the seesaw, sending that goal up and out of reach—initially.

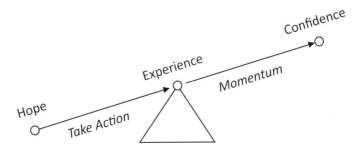

That means that everyone has an uphill battle to get up the incline toward success. No matter how little you bring in terms of Doubt, your inexperience will still be enough to tip the empty scales, and that will mean that you will have to climb up toward your goal. It doesn't matter what advantages or disadvantages you think you have in life, everyone has an uphill battle to become his or her best self. The key, then, is to not stop climbing until you reach your goal.

Don't get distracted because you think someone else started further ahead or because you think that your climb is steeper. It's the same process for all of us, and our individual Core Whys are uniquely suited to shape and complete the climbs we want to achieve. Forget everyone else and focus on you. The playing field was level until you came along. Now it's up to you to overcome the challenges by Taking Action so that you can move onward and upward.

Summary

I've sat in the same room with millionaires and even billionaires before. I don't tell you this to make you think I'm one of the cool kids, but because I want you to see how this principle of Taking Action works. In all the people I've met, I have yet to meet anyone "rich" who inherited all the money. Those people exist, I'm sure, but they are a lot fewer and farther between than you probably think. There's a reason that so many lottery winners end up more broke and worse off a short time after winning. They never had to Take Action, and therefore still don't really know how. Successful people do. Without the principle of Action, you can't expect success and growth.

Michelangelo, the famous painter and sculptor, is reported to have said, "If people knew how hard I had to work to gain my mastery, it would not seem so wonderful at all." He was summarizing this chapter for us. All worthy endeavors take considerable Action. We don't wake up in the morning and have lightning strike to make us suddenly successful. We have to push forward day after day if we want to reach our full potential. From the inside, having seen all the Action that went into a specific goal, it loses all its mystical wonder. You can see the inner workings and the path that you've traveled. Maintaining realistic perspective is one of the keys to humility as well. It's only when seen from the outside—devoid of all the ups and downs—that the path to success seems straight, or unfair.

Remember, your Hope will buoy you up and push you along if you will get your neocortex in line and Take Action. Set your goals, break them down into actionable parts, and then get moving. Find your Hope, then move your feet. As you do, you'll gain Experience—our next topic—and be well on your way toward becoming the person you've always wanted to be.

EXPERIENCE

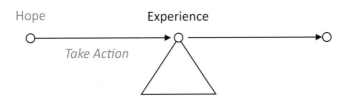

Experience - [ik-speer-ee-uh ns]
- n. - a particular instance of personally encountering or undergoing something
- v.t. - to have experience of; meet with; undergo; feel[7]

What is Experience? In the most basic sense, Experience is simply the result of any Action you take. When you do something, something will happen (even if that "something" turns out to be basically nothing), and that becomes your Experience. Experience is also the sum total of all the things you've been through in your life. Experience can be good or bad in terms of how it makes you feel, but it can always be leveraged to make you a better person and it can never be taken from you.

Experiential Reality

If Experience is simply what you're left with when the chips fall where they will, what good is Experience to you? To answer that question, I have to ask you another question. What good is Taking Action?

---

[7] experience. Dictionary.com.*Dictionary.com Unabridged.* Random House, Inc. http://dictionary.reference.com/browse/experience (accessed: February 11, 2015).

The two answers are actually the same. You see, whenever you Take Action, something will happen (even if that something really is nothing). For example, when you go out to your car to head off to work in the morning (or the store), you put the key in and turn it. What happens? It starts, right? That's an experience, and that experience teaches you to Believe that your car will start when you turn the key. What happens, however, if you have an older car and it's really cold this morning? Is it possible that the car won't start? Actually, the cold can decrease the efficacy of your battery and make it possible that the car really won't start—especially in lower-efficiency, older vehicles.

If you turn the key and nothing happens, you still gain experience though. You gain the experience of having your car *not* do exactly what you expect from it. What you do next will depend on who you are—which is largely based on the accumulation of all the Experiences you've gained in life and how you've interpreted those things. If you have lots of Experience in dealing with cars that don't always function as expected, you might Take Action by trying to troubleshoot in an effort to find and fix the problem. If, however, you have no such Experience, you are more likely to call someone who does have that kind of experience—a father, spouse, sibling, child, friend, or mechanic.

Whether or not you would personally try to attack the problem highlights the Belief Blueprint perfectly. Confidence is born from Experience, Experience is gained by Taking Action, and we Take Action when we Hope that there is something worth gaining and Believe that we can gain it. In a way, you could say that Confidence is like having a critical mass of Experience in a given endeavor. Since everything you do will give you Experience, you can look at this as meaning that everything you do is taking you closer to confidence in some facet of your life—so long as you really are *doing* something. You can't build Confidence without Taking Action.

Of course, even choosing to do nothing will fill your life with a certain type of Experience. It'll be the Experience of nothingness, but even that is Experience of a kind. Those feelings could even help drive you to Take Action in the future if you ever tire of feeling empty.

The good news is, once you gain Experience, it's yours forever. You can't ever lose it. This can seem like a negative for some people who have particularly traumatic events in their lives, but even those Experiences can actually work for your good if you look at them in the right light. We'll talk more about how to make your Experiences work for you, but for now I just need you to understand that they're yours forever.

In a way, you can consider them like a 401k. As you go through life, you accrue Experience into your experiential retirement account. When you change directions or pick up a new goal, you can roll over your experiential 401k to your new focus, just like changing employers. Those Experiences are yours forever, and I'll show you why that's a good thing.

Driver's Ed

When you were learning how to drive a car, did you think you could pull it off? Did you honestly think you could learn how to control hundreds of horsepower and thousands of pounds of materials to go where you wanted, when you wanted, and all by pushing on a couple different metal flaps with your feet and turning a plastic circle with your hands? Sounds ridiculous, right? Yet that's what you do every time you drive a car—and that's just for the automatic transmissions. Manual transmission takes driving to a whole new level of complexity.

Why did you think you could drive that car? I'll tell you that you felt like you could drive the car—or at least learn how—because of all your previous Experience and Confidence. Everything else you'd ever learned or done all came together to help you Hope and Believe that you could learn this new skill. Learning addition back in grade school? Yup. Writing that English paper? Yup. That goal you scored in little-league soccer? Yes, that too. Every little Experience in your life has built up your belief in yourself and resulted in a Hope that you could learn to drive.

And not just your direct, personal Experiences either. You'd been watching your parents drive for years. You watched your older siblings (if you have any). Maybe you even watched your friends if any of them were old enough to get a permit or license before you. Certainly you'd seen people drive on TV at least a few times. All of those Experiences factored in too.

All your Experiences had taught you that you could learn. They may not have taught you exactly how to operate several thousand pounds of metal propelled by hundreds of horsepower, but they gave you Confidence in their own right and helped you to Hope that you could learn this new skill. Think about it, would you have felt as positive about learning if you'd never done anything else in your life? If you hadn't been through the struggle of learning to walk, run, jump, do math, ride a bike, talk, and so on?

Every Action you take affects the balance on hundreds or even thousands of little individual Belief Blueprints—each model reflecting a different tiny fraction of your life. You may be consciously focusing on working toward a specific goal, but each step closer will help you feel more Confident—increasing your Belief about yourself in all the other aspects of your life. You can think about it in terms of how achieving that goal will boost your overall perception of yourself and help you have more Confidence in your ability to achieve the next goal. The reality is that just moving closer to a goal can have that effect. Allow me to demonstrate.

Manual Transmission

You learned on a specific car, right? Maybe a cheap one in connection with driver's ed? Once you felt comfortable with driving that car, how did you feel about the next car you got in? If it was a BMW or Lexus, you might have been nervous about the value of the vehicle, but did you doubt your ability to drive it? Probably not. The Experience you already had from driving that Corolla or Civic or whatever was enough to nearly tip the scales for you already. You may have had to search for the headlights or gear shifter or wipers, but you already knew you could drive the car once you tracked down the familiar control mechanisms.

What if you were then put in a big pickup or SUV? You were probably concerned by the size of the vehicle, but you probably weren't concerned with the interface or being able to drive. However, if you learned in an automatic, how do you think you'd feel with being thrown into a vehicle with a manual transmission? If you've already learned how to drive a manual, think back to how you felt. Terrified anyone?

There's a third pedal? And what's with the pole sticking out of the floor of the car (assuming it wasn't an older 3-on-the-tree manual). Now you have to think about more than just stop and go and steer. Now you have to worry about being in the right gear and how to switch between gears. It's an added layer of complexity, and it requires more Experience in order to tip the scales. Again, though, once you're comfortable driving manual in one car, you can switch to pretty much any other car and still be comfortable. The Experience goes with you.

In fact, I know a guy with a manual transmission, 3/4 ton pickup from 1985. He tells me he's going to make his kids learn how to drive in that vehicle, and he's going to do it for two reasons. First, the truck is practically a tank, so the kids will be safe from anything short of a nuclear bomb inside it (though I'm less confident about everything outside the truck). Second, it's supposedly a difficult vehicle to drive, and this guy knows that his kids will be able to drive almost anything after learning how to drive that truck. They'll understand manual transmissions and manual everything else, so they'll be able to handle and appreciate all of the modern advances and conveniences that make driving easier.

Be an Experience Collector

The point of all this is to help you realize the importance of becoming something of an Experience collector. You want to hoard up Experience at every opportunity because you never know when it'll come back to help you—even if your latest goal seems entirely unrelated.

Now, this doesn't mean that you need to go out and "experience" the world and everything it has to offer. I don't mean that you need to go travel or try exotic things. You don't need to try skydiving or the luge or BMX racing or anything. What I *do* mean is that you shouldn't go out of your way to avoid things that tie in to your goals. When you have the chance to do something new, don't find an excuse to sit it out (unless it violates your morals, laws of the land, or plain common sense). Instead, treasure up the opportunities when they come.

We've talked about Hope and Belief and Taking Action, and you know that you need to move your feet in order to get from where you are to wherever you want to go. Every journey requires some amount of Action (resulting in Experience) in order to get from start to finish. The amount of additional Experience you need for each new goal depends on how similar your past experience is. What's cool about this is that you never know just how many journeys the Experience you just gained will work for. It'll help you now, but it'll also help to advance you in the future, to give you a head start on future endeavors and goals. In this light it's easier to see the value of formal education, not only the things you learn, but the Experience of learning.

So treasure up all the Experience you find because it will all enrich you and make you better than you were before in some way. That said, there are some cautions you should be aware of before you go acquiring Experience with reckless abandon. Experience is best gained by working toward a goal or end of some kind. This goes back to the concept of having a direction. If you just run around seeking random Experiences, what overall purpose will you really be moving toward? How will that be reinforcing your Why or taking you toward your What? Don't get caught up thinking that Experience is the end goal. It is the only means to the ends we seek.

Don't just pursue Experience at random for the sole sake of gaining more Experience. Instead, gain the Experience by actively pursuing your goals and aspirations. Taking Action on your goals is the best way to help you gain relevant Experience anyway—Experience that shapes you in accordance with your Core Why. With that in mind, I want to give you a caution to remember when you embark on particularly difficult goals.

The Crucible of Experience

We've already discussed how your presence on the left side of the Belief Blueprint is what shifts it from a nice, even playing field into the mountain climb you go through to get to the end destination. Your Hope and positive Experiences empower you to climb, but your Doubts and negative Experiences weigh down on that bench and start you at a low point. This relationship between positive and negative Experience serves as a sort of balancing act as you undertake a goal. If you build up more positive Experience than negative Experience, you can reach the middle of the seesaw and cause it to tip in your favor.

If, on the other hand, you focus on more negative Experience than positive, it can actually build up and encourage you to stall in your efforts to push forward. You'll basically be adding weight to yourself as you try to climb, making it harder and harder to move forward. For this reason, I sometimes call the balancing act the Crucible of Experience, and it's the place where mere good intentions go to die.

A crucible is a dish of some kind used to melt down an element— usually a metal. Typically, the crucible is made of ceramic or some other material that can withstand extreme temperatures without melting or deforming. The metal or other substance in the crucible is usually something valuable (like gold or silver) but can also be something impure. The whole purpose of a crucible is to separate out the impurities from a substance in order to make it more useful. That's another good reason to call the acquisition of Experience a crucible. By gaining experience, you will be purifying yourself.

It's important to understand how the process works, however, because it's not an easy one—not when worthy goals are involved anyway. Metal is refined by placing the impure ore in the crucible and then applying intense heat. As the temperature climbs, different materials will begin to separate out. Some things will fizzle away as gasses; others will rise to the surface as liquid or solid waste products. Eventually, you'll have siphoned off all the waste and be able to pull the pure metal from the crucible.

Interestingly, you can't refine metal without sitting and watching it. You have to stay focused or you'll ruin what you're trying to do. The reason is that the metal you're trying to refine will typically melt at a lower temperature than some of the contaminants. If you leave it unattended, the temperature can go up too much, melt those other waste products, mix with the metal, and ruin the whole thing. At that point, you'd have to let the whole thing cool and try again from the beginning—assuming the metal wasn't permanently ruined already.

Undergoing change works much the same way. If you try to just let yourself "develop" in the background, you'll soon find that you have gotten contaminated by things you never intended. You may not purge all of the things holding you back—and you may put yourself through more challenges than necessary to achieve your goals. While facing extra challenges isn't necessarily a bad thing, it will slow you down by making your growth take longer.

Instead, you need to take an active hand in your growth and stay watchful and in control throughout the process. The crucible is hard enough all on its own. It represents all the inevitable difficulties, setbacks, and challenges you'll face on your journey toward self-improvement, and nearly any worthy goal will have plenty of those learning opportunities along the way. If you aren't taking control of the process and moving forward with conscious effort, you run the risk of adding even more challenges by virtue of your negligence. You can get through to the other side and come out pure, but only if you're committed. If your commitment wavers, you will run the risk of getting burned up in the process. That's why you need to go in recognizing the difficulty ahead but without fearing that difficulty.

Good Intention Graveyard

Earlier, I mentioned that the crucible is where good intentions go to die. Let me explain that here. All of us have good intentions in our lives. For some people, these are just the passing thoughts of helping other people; for others, good intentions rule their lives and run them from one worthy endeavor to another. Now let me make a distinction. You can have good intentions for something or you can have a good goal. What's the difference?

A good goal is something that retains your focus because it's driven by your Why. You put in conscious effort and keep that thing at the top of your to-do list. You think about it frequently and make a point of taking steps forward toward completion of the goal. For a real goal, as we discussed earlier, you'll have a plan of attack—a game plan. You'll be Taking Action on it regularly, and probably as often as possible.

A good intention is only some of those things. A good intention is something in which you see value but not something in which you see *enough* value to make a concerted effort at accomplishing the task or gaining the skill. It might align with your Why, or it might not. It might just sound like a nice What. For some people, a good intention will be more of an altruistic focus which returns no real personal benefit. You know you probably should do it—or maybe even want to do it—but you have too much else going on to make it the top priority right now.

Ultimately, you will expend your effort and time to move forward on your goals, not your intentions. Your intentions will sit at the bottom of your priority list and languish. This is a dangerous place to be for anything worthwhile because there's a chance you might get started on that thing but then not have the drive to see it through to completion. Once you start on a task, you start work on the Belief Blueprint. That begins a process of either moving forward or moving backward. If you are putting in the time and effort, you will move forward—however quickly or slowly that might be. If you don't make the time to focus on it, however, you will simply begin backsliding.

Eventually, you will backslide far enough that any Hope you once had will turn to Despair. Any Belief you once had will fade into Apathy. You'll lose your motivation, and it will be that much easier to just keep putting that thing off indefinitely. This is why good intentions—worthwhile endeavors that you don't make time for right now—tend to die in the crucible. Without your focus, they get buried under everything else. Since you aren't there to mind the crucible, the metal will likely get contaminated and ruined. Surviving the crucible is not a passive process. You need to be awake and alert to make it through. You need to be aware of yourself.

For that reason, there are two things you need to keep in mind when it comes to surviving the crucible. Obviously, there are more than just two things you need to be thinking about, but these two are blanket statements that apply to all goals and opportunities. Other things you keep in mind will be more specific to the goal you are pursuing. So, in addition to everything else, keep these two things in mind. First, your Why needs to be stronger than "Why Not?" Second, you need to enter with the intent to exit.

Limbic Opposition

The crucible is a harsh, unforgiving environment. It's that very hardship which serves to give you the Experience you need to progress. If the crucible were easy—if there weren't any opposition like we talked about in the chapter about Hope—then you would never stretch yourself. You would never grow. Growth only happens when you buckle down and overcome resistance. You *want* the crucible to be hard because that's how you prove yourself—by coming through it alive. The stronger the resistance, the stronger it will make you when you overcome it.

The problem is, as I just mentioned, that harshness will wear away at your resolve. If you are only casual about something, the crucible will melt you down in no time. Even strong resolve can be worn away eventually. All it takes is time and a bit of carelessness on your part. If you can't ever convince yourself to make it to the end and finish, you'll eventually be worn down under the weight and pressure.

Sometimes, people make goals and then begin working toward those goals without ever really thinking about what they're doing and what the process will entail—what it will demand. This most often happens in public settings when you see your peers making a certain type of goal and want to follow suit. You may even get pumped up by some kind of motivational presentation and set a big, worthwhile goal…and then go home.

Have you ever had that happen? You make a goal that feels impossible at the time but you decide that you'll just power through? That's not necessarily a bad thing. Plenty of worthwhile goals will seem beyond your reach when you make them. In fact, most goals worth achieving aren't immediately within reach. That's why they're called goals. You already know you're going to have to work toward them. You'll Take Action and gain Experience and grow, rising to the demands of the goal. The real issue here is when the goal is out of reach *and* you don't necessarily care deeply about it. This is the result when your Why isn't fully aligned.

As you know, your true Why is what will drive you. It must be stronger than your desire to just try anything to survive. "Why not give it a shot?" This thought is very different than the focused and Why-driven, "I must do this." If you're not fully aligned with your Why, then you will unintentionally allow the opposition to win over time— not by stopping you in your tracks, but by distracting you to work on things that speak more directly to your true Why. This is one of the best descriptions of what it means to "spin your wheels." Not being fully committed to the right outcome may even lead you to do some things that you feel are disingenuous or even contrary to your values. In this light it's probably no surprise to learn that this natural opposition lives in your limbic brain right alongside your Why. It's how our limbic brain sabotages activities that don't remedy your immediate deepest needs.

A good example of how this plays out is thinking about preparing for retirement. So many people don't do it, yet everyone knows how important it is. No one wants to get near the end of his or her life and still be working to scrape by. Many of us want to still be working, but we want to be working for other reasons or causes, not just to make ends meet. So why don't people put more time and effort into preparing for retirement? There's limbic opposition in play.

When you get your paycheck, does it ever feel a bit small? Do you ever have more month left at the end of the money? Many people do. In that situation, how can you justify putting money aside for the future? You need it right now. Your Why tells you that you want to be ready for retirement, but limbic opposition says you'd rather get a loaf of bread and a gallon of milk for your kids. It's a difficult situation.

You'll have opposition in almost every goal you ever make. Sometimes it'll be weak; sometimes strong. Weak or strong, count on opposition. The key is to make sure that your Why is stronger—strong enough to overcome the natural opposition and push you forward to success. To do that, you'll need to really dig deep and examine your priorities. What is most important to you, and how can you alter the situation so that it aligns with your Why? When you choose a goal that pits your Why against other basic needs, you're setting at least one of those needs up for failure—and you'll experience a lot of emotional turmoil along the way.

Instead, align your Why before you move forward. Make sure your goals won't interfere with your core. You don't want to end up being your own worst enemy.

Enter with the Intent to Exit

In addition to making sure that you're playing for the right team (that you're in line with your Core Why), you can minimize the chance that your intentions will die in the crucible by making sure to enter the crucible with the intent to exit. If you're not fully committed to something, don't start it. As John Wooden, hall of fame basketball player and coach, said, "If you don't have time to do it right, when will you have time to do it over?"

All too often, we throw ourselves at noble goals but do so casually. We aren't fully engaged in the process. We have good intentions, but we don't really have the bandwidth. This is why you want to be careful about just how many goals you set for yourself at a time. It's better to buckle down and really get traction on a few solid goals than to try to spread yourself thin across a whole multitude of different things. There's an old saying that you have "too many irons in the fire." It's a blacksmithing quote that refers to heating up iron bars in order to make them malleable before working on them. If you put too many irons in the fire, the fire itself may be smothered and you'll probably lose track of what you're doing with each bar. Leaving them unattended too long can ruin them as well.

It's better to just keep additional goals in mind or on a list rather than starting too many all at the same time. You want to be able to focus your efforts on a few things, enter the crucible on those things, push through the refining process, and come out the other side with new Experience and Momentum to propel you through the next endeavor. If you enter casually or too many times simultaneously, you'll end up bogging yourself down. You won't have the bandwidth to focus on all your different initiatives, and some of them will burn out, leaving you feeling like a failure instead of a success. That feeling will then weigh down your hope in all your other endeavors—current and future.

This is why you can't afford to start on a path unless you intend to see it through. You can be casual and still go through all the right motions, but they won't be enough. You'll have all the right mechanisms in place to help you Take Action and gain Experience, but you won't really want the end result—or maybe you *do* want it, but you're scared of what will happen to you if you're successful. Either way, if you can't keep yourself engaged, you're far more likely to experience failure than you are to find success.

When an initiative dies in the crucible of Experience, it dies by Despair—and that's not something you want to encourage in your life. Intentions die when your Hope erodes away, leaving you to face the fire of refinement on your own. Your willpower may be strong, but the neocortex isn't built for that kind of protracted effort. Your neocortex is a sprinter. It can do amazing work over short spans of time. Most goals, however, are marathons. They need the staying power and endurance of the limbic brain. They need the power of Hope—the Hope that you'll be able to complete the journey. So don't start on something unless you intend to finish it. There's no reason to set yourself up for failure by being casual about your goals.

All Ores Are Created Unequally

One final note on the Crucible of Experience: all ores are created unequally. The amount of time required in the crucible in order to be refined properly depends on the purity of the ore going in. If an ore is 99 percent gold and only 1 percent impurity, it won't take very long to get out the impurities and have a pure metal. If, on the other hand, you're a little more normal and have more like 30 percent gold and 70 percent impurity, it will take a while longer. You'll be investing a lot more time and effort into reaching your end destination. The good news is that even if you're 1 percent gold and 99 percent impurity, you can still reach your goal; it's just going to take that much more time and effort to get there, so you need to be ready for an uphill battle.

Here's another reason why this matters. You never know exactly where you stand in relation to a goal until you start moving toward it, and you never know where someone else stands either. Let's put it this way. You and your friend both decide it's time to get back in shape. You've been putting it off, and you're going to step up and be accountability partners for each other. You've rallied your Why around the ability to keep up with your children thanks to some newfound cardiovascular fitness; your friend is all about the financial savings of being healthy instead of visiting the doctor. Your Whys are different, but you're both engaged. You decide to Take Action by starting a couch-to-5k program that will start you out at a low, slow level but move you up at regular intervals until you can run a little over three miles (five kilometers) without stopping.

You agree to do the program together to help keep each other motivated. On the first day, you're both huffing and puffing halfway through the segment, but you can see how it's possible for you to eventually build up your stamina and fitness. You know you've got a long way to go, but your Why is strong and the Experience is building your Belief. Halfway through the program, though, you notice that your friend seems to be making progress more quickly than you.

Turns out, your friend was on the soccer team back in high school and played in a city league up until just a couple years ago. You, on the other hand, haven't really ever done any running except if something was chasing you. Your friend, in terms of the crucible, started out at a higher level of refinement than you did. That doesn't mean that your friend will reach the destination first; it just means that you'll need to put in more effort to get to the same place. If you're willing to put in that extra effort as you go, you can still arrive together. Otherwise, your friend will "finish" first, and you'll need a little extra time to make up the difference—not that that's a problem. You just need to be aware of that possibility so that it doesn't depress you if it happens.

Risks of Comparison

You and your friend started out as different compositions of ore. Your friend was already more refined because of past Experience from all those years playing soccer. You didn't have that Experience to build from, so you required different levels of effort to complete the refining process. You will never be the exact same composition as any other person for any task. This is important to note because, as humans, we seem to build our individual realities around comparisons. I'm smarter than that person; I'm not as smart as that one. I'm more attractive than that person but not that one. My house is bigger or smaller. I'm thinner or larger. And the list goes on.

This tendency to compare ourselves to others when we frame our perception of reality can expose us to a very serious danger. If you're not careful, you will tend to compare yourself to people whose ore is further along in the refinement process than your own. Comparing yourself to others this way—comparing things you're working on to things others are already better at—can be very disheartening. Frequently, it will lead you to question whether what you're doing is actually a good idea or not. After all, if everyone else seems to already be so much further along, why should you even bother?

For this reason, you can't afford to compare yourself to other people. As we've established, everyone's Experience is different. Everyone's Why is different. Trying to compare your merits with someone else isn't even comparing apples and oranges (which are at least both fruits); it's more like comparing apples and bicycles. They're completely different in pretty much every way. So don't compare yourself to others and potentially impact your Why for no reason. You can go to others for advice and assistance, but there's nothing you can really do about where you stand in comparison to others (aside from moving yourself forward).

Along the same lines, you're not the exact same composition of ore for each of your different, personal undertakings either. One thing might come easily to you while another seems to escape your understanding for years. You might understand and love piano but be totally baffled by the intricacies of organic chemistry. You might love marketing but hate finance—or vice versa. You might love public speaking but dread actually writing anything longer than a text message. Your unique Experience will uniquely prepare you for different things in life. Don't be discouraged when you run into a situation where nothing you've done before seems to have helped in any way. That's normal too.

Be patient with yourself. Some things will come easily, but some won't. Some will require more time and effort in the crucible before you're ready to come out. Don't let that impact your Hope and turn you to Despair. I can't tell you how many people I've seen try to pick up a new skill only to quit just as they're starting to get the hang of it—all because they weren't seeing the results they wanted as quickly as they expected. In a lot of ways, Experience builds in a sort of exponential fashion—and we'll talk more about that in the chapter about Momentum. This means that the growth happens more quickly later on, after you've already built the foundation. Don't stop building the house once you are finally ready to make some headway.

Weight of Experience

A big reason people quit just before breaking through is because of something I call the Weight of Experience. In the grand scheme of building experience, some things count for more than other things. When it comes to sculpting a beautiful statue out of marble, for instance, your skill with painting or even wood carving will mean more than your skill for business negotiations or your skill in making friends. The more closely related your past Experience is to your newest venture, the more weight it will carry.

If you're good at making friends, that will boost your Belief and initial Hope with regards to asking someone out on a date. You already know you can meet new people and engage them in conversation, and that's a big part of dating. You know you can be polite and thoughtful, and those are key characteristics to have in the dating world too. You're already a big part of the way there—just like knowing how to drive an automatic car and then trying to learn a manual transmission—but there are still some things you aren't sure about, and that will become the seesaw in the Belief Blueprint. Until you've gained Experience with actual dating, you will be operating on your Belief and Hope, not on real Confidence. You'll be relying on related Experience depending on the individual weights of those different Experiences.

But there's another aspect to the weight of Experience that is important to note. Not all Experience from the crucible is equally relevant to new ventures and, more importantly, not all Experience relates positively—at least, not without some thought. The Experience you gain in the crucible comes in two general varieties and is based almost entirely on your perception. There is positive and negative. How you interpret the Experiences you have can depend largely on your personality (remember our discussion of optimists versus pessimists), but it largely depends on whether or not you feel like you moved forward as a result of a given Action.

Some Experiences are easy to see. You suggested a course of action in a business meeting, people agreed, and the team acted on it. That feels like success. You bought a present for your niece, and she loved it. Success again. On the other hand, you tried to repair the car radiator and it exploded and damaged other components of the car. Failure (sort of; we'll talk about this again in a moment). You bought a nice lotion for your spouse only to find out that they are allergic to one of the ingredients. Failure again. Or is it?

The Crucible of Experience will fill you with Experiences of both the positive and negative varieties, and how those things weigh out will determine when you reach the point of critical mass in the Belief Blueprint. When you sit down on the teeter-totter, you take it crashing down to the ground. The weight of your Doubts brings it down because you don't yet have enough Experience to go up and over. However, your past positive Experiences lighten your load by counterbalancing the negative, which makes it easier to climb. Build up enough positive Experience and you'll tip through the next chapter as you gain Momentum on your way to Confidence. New negative Experiences can weigh you down further. Build up enough bad Experience and you'll start to erode your Hope. The crucible will eventually burn up your good intentions and you'll end up in Despair.

The good news is that having some bad Experiences early on doesn't mean that you are doomed to failure. In fact, there's an interesting psychological phenomenon which actually encourages you to forget past problems more quickly than you would forget something positive. This is a valuable, natural tool in your toolbox, so let's learn a little more about it.

Fading Affect Bias

This human tendency to forget the bad things and remember the good ones is one of the things that has kept us from falling into Despair as a race. Because negative things fade over time, we can move on beyond them to grow and improve. In a way, you can look at this as an evolutionary advancement. It's solid proof that as long as you're still alive, things can always get better. I once heard a second-hand account of a family that was planning an activity together and they were trying to figure out how to accommodate their 90-year-old grandmother who would be attending. When she found out about the thoughtful arrangements they had been coming up with to keep her comfortable, she quickly affirmed, "I'm not dead yet! I'll be fine!" What grandma was really trying to say, is that as long as we're living, there is still a chance to find Hope despite opposition.

If we were programmed to think back to all the times that trying something new resulted in disaster, we would never try anything new. Think of all the advancements we've had as a human family because people weren't willing to accept failure and stop. They pushed on against the odds and we enjoy the fruits of their labors today—and I don't just mean things like the light bulb or airplane. Even simple, basic advancements like fire and the wheel undoubtedly took patience for the trial-and-error process. Where would we be today without those things?

This tendency to forget bad Experiences more quickly than we forget good ones is important enough that it actually has an official name: the Fading Affect Bias. Since that string of terms is very academic in its origin and usage, let's define it briefly, starting with affect. Affect, in psychological research, basically means emotion. Bias is the show of favoritism, and you already know what it means when something fades. With that understanding, the fading affect bias is really something like the "use of bias in determining which emotions fade first."

In essence the limbic brain prefers to hold on to positive things and let go of negative ones, so that's exactly what it will do. When you have an Experience (really a string of Experiences over a short space of time), your limbic brain is more likely to retain the emotions you gain from the positive Experiences—those that served your most prevalent needs—and forget the others. This is why you can go on vacation and have so many bad things happen that you swear you'll never leave home again, yet a month later, you're reminiscing about how wonderful it was. You forget about how the hotel messed up your room reservation or how the pool was closed for half your stay. Instead, you remember all the good parts of the trip—the time you spent with family and friends, the activities you did, and the memories you made. In fact, the whole idea of "making memories" (which has a positive connotation) is dependent on the fading affect bias because almost nothing happens in life without a few hiccups along the way. Fading affect bias helps you remember the good stuff and forget those hiccups.

Psychologists began looking at fading affect bias back in the 1930s by interviewing people and asking them to recount life experiences like weddings, birthdays, and holiday seasons. Then, just a few weeks after the initial interview, the researchers would go back to the people and do a follow up interview. The second interview was unannounced and came as a surprise for the participants. In the second interview, the researchers found that recall for negative experiences had dropped off much more sharply than recall of positive ones.

Since that almost accidental discovery, researchers have made fading affect bias a topic of study. Time and time again, they've found that people tend to remember positive Experiences in more detail and for a longer period of time than negative Experiences. This is good news for us because it means that there's still Hope even when you start on a journey and suffer a string of setbacks right off the bat. As you continue down the road, you'll forget those setbacks more quickly than you would forget a positive Experience. This relationship means that you can suffer early failure without totally losing the will to continue. Even better, by the end of the journey, you might not remember the setbacks at all—or at least won't remember how much they set you back.

Fading affect bias helps to swing the scales of Experience in your favor. It helps to diminish the weight of negative Experience from holding you back, even offloading it over time, while helping you retain the positive Experience that moves you forward. Do you remember when we discussed the advantages of being an optimist versus being a pessimist? The fading affect bias shows that we're hardwired to be optimists, and it can really help out in making optimism our reality. Obviously, the neocortex can still screen out the positive and only feed on the negative, but that becomes a conscious choice on your part. The limbic brain would rather focus on positive things and use that positivity to drive progress and development.

Turning the Page

And the fading affect bias isn't the only tool you can use to improve your outlook on life. This next tool isn't necessarily easy, but a master of this technique can triumph over just about anything else that life throws in the way. The reality of the world around us is that most of us don't like to be confronted with negative events. We prefer to be happy, not angry, depressed, or miserable. For that reason, we are shocked when something gruesome or awful presents itself. Certain elements of society—out of a craving for attention—have capitalized on this human nature in order to take as much attention as they can get. You can probably think of people or organizations like this.

And, even without those people and organizations, undeniably bad things still happen to us. No matter who you are or where you stand on the socio-economic ladder, bad things will happen. Add that to the way society tries to shock us with negativity and you have a situation in which it's frighteningly easy to get depressed and discouraged. It's hard to maintain Hope and Belief in the face of that kind of attack, but there is a way. You can learn to change the way you view those negative events so that you see them in a positive light. Allow me to demonstrate this by telling you a story from my childhood.

First Water

When I was about 11 years old, I was part of a scouting group in Arizona where I lived. We met once a week or so and did merit-badge requirements, went on the occasional campout, and did things 11 year-olds do; i.e., stupid stuff. Still the leaders were well meaning enough and tried hard to help us learn and grow; we just weren't the most receptive audience all the time.

At one point, my scout leader decided that we should do a day hike through the Superstition Mountains east of Phoenix. We were going to go on a hike from First Water to Second Water, just over 12-miles by the map. That's a pretty long hike for some 11-year-old boys, so we made sure to plan ahead, and we brought some extra adults with us. My scout leader had a military background, so the idea of a long hike wasn't particularly concerning to him. The assistant scout leader, on the other hand, was a great guy but was badly out of shape in addition to being about 100 pounds overweight. We all knew that he wasn't ready for that kind of hike, but he was convinced that he could just tough it out and then spend some time in recovery afterward. My dad also came along for the hike. He wasn't really a scout leader, but he was looking forward to the exercise, some beautiful scenery, and the time with me.

My actual scout leader had only recently moved to the area, so he got a map from someone else to show us the route to take. It wasn't a topographic map, but it showed the zig-line that we'd need to take and had labels for different trail markers and landmarks to help us make sure we were on the right track. Now, to be fair, this was back before the days of GPS and satellite imaging. We couldn't just Google the trail and get a map that way because Google didn't actually exist back then. Nowadays, you can practically "walk" the trail by just going to Google Earth and following the route of the hike. We didn't have that option. We had to do things the old-fashioned way; we had to track down a map and talk to people who thought they knew how to explain the route.

We planned the hike for a Saturday in early November when the weather would be nicer—keep in mind that we were living in Arizona at the time. Daytime temperatures in the rugged desert mountains were in the 70s and it got down into the 50s at night. When we got to the trailhead to start the hike, we had a clear sky and good sun overhead. We'd packed plenty of water, some lunch, and a few snacks for along the way. We were young, but we knew we were going on a long hike. Everyone had good shoes and plenty of supplies. So let's tie this back in for a second.

Thinking back to the model, our Hope was to prove that we could do something difficult. We were going to make that a reality by completing the goal of hiking from First Water to Second Water. Our first Actions were to get a map and plan the route, date, and time. Next we gathered the necessary supplies and got ourselves the appropriate gear. Once we had Taken those preliminary Actions, we were ready for the next step of actually starting on the hike.

Now, I'd actually hiked First Water before, though I can't remember when, so at some point along the path, I started to realize that things didn't feel quite right. There was something different about the trail—something unfamiliar. For whatever reason, I felt like we were going the wrong way. Still, my scout leader had a map, and we were following it. I didn't see a reason to question his strategy when it seemed to be getting us to where we wanted to go.

At one point, the trail got really steep and spotty, like parts of it were gone. We'd go for a while and then have to look around for the next piece of the trail. It was disconcerting and worrying, but we weren't going to let it stop us from achieving our goal. We'd expected hardship along the way. We ended up going up and over a small mountain and then coming down the backside. As we did, we caught sight of another trail below and we could see some of the other major landmarks in the area (like Weaver's Needle, a natural stone obelisk that rose a few hundred feet from the desert floor), so we figured we'd just been told about an older version of the trail and now we were coming back to the real trail. We kept going, figuring that we were on track.

Getting Lost

We kept pushing forward, but things started to look sketchy. For one thing, we kept expecting a turn that never came. At some point the trail was supposed to turn off and take us down to a riverbed, but the trail just kept going. The trail we were following no longer matched up with the map my scout leader had. Landmarks weren't where they were supposed to be. Turns weren't where they were supposed to be. We were following the plan, but the plan wasn't following our reality, and we were quickly approaching a serious, dangerous situation. That's when we realized something. On the trail, all the markers were numeric (1, 2, 3, and so on); on the map, the markers were alphabetic (A, B, C, and so on). In light of that, it wasn't all that surprising that we'd been reading the map incorrectly.

That's when we realized that we had taken a wrong turn at some point and were no longer on the trail we thought we were on. We had planned on a 12-mile hike, but we were on the trail for a 30-mile hike—a hike which would take us past daylight and into the dark. Sure enough, the sun started dropping to the horizon long before we saw our destination. Now, if we'd known that we were going to do a 30-mile hike, we would have prepared for it and paced ourselves better (or not gone, as is more likely; most of us were just kids). That wasn't the case, however. We had planned on a 12-mile hike, and we'd rationed our supplies accordingly. We had also planned on a day hike, so we hadn't brought flashlights, tents, sleeping bags, or any other night gear. Some of us didn't even have sweatshirts because you don't need a sweatshirt when it's 70 degrees and sunny. You don't need long sleeves until it's 50 degrees, you're covered in sweat, and it's nighttime.

Owing to an unrelated experience earlier in my childhood, at that point in my life I was prone to occasional panic attacks and severe anxiety (maybe another reason my dad had come along). I'd had a baby sister almost choke to death, and the Experience had left me a nervous child. When the sun started going down and the end of the trail was nowhere in sight, I started to get really nervous. Thankfully my dad was there. I don't know how I would have been without him there to calm me. That didn't change the fact that we were lost in the middle of nowhere with dwindling supplies, fading light, and no idea of how to get home. My dad helped me to stay in control, but I was still freaking out—as were most of the other kids.

At that point, my scout leader decided that the best thing for us to do was to follow a dry stream bed downhill. His thought was that, at some point, the stream bed would have to cross over the trail for Second Water and take us out to our destination. So we started down. For the first few hours after the sun went down, things got very tricky. We had one tiny flashlight (more by chance than by design), but it ran out of batteries before long, and then we were left in the dark. Eventually, the moon came up and we were able to better see where we were going. Thankfully, because we were in the riverbed now, the chance of running into dangerous or hazardous things was much smaller. We were basically walking down a path of loose sand rather than over and around the rocks and cacti we'd been walking next to all day.

The terrain wasn't the only challenge though. We ran into several rattlesnakes, but they warned us when we got close, giving us a chance to go around them. We also had kids pushed past the point of exhaustion. Some were just fine but others were hallucinating or feeling sick because of the effort. A few of us got really quiet and kind of listless. Most of us weren't really physically in shape for a 12-mile hike, much less a 30-mile one, but we'd all figured that we'd just tough it out and then relax for a while—just like our overweight and out of shape assistant leader. As for him, he was really bad off. He wasn't vocal about it like us boys, but he'd probably have had trouble with a 3-mile hike. Hiking just hadn't ever been a focus for him. I think it actually took him a week or more to recover from accompanying us on that hike.

Thankfully, my scout leader was right about discovering the trail to find our way home. We followed the riverbed down until about two in the morning before we found the trail to take us out to Second Water. That happened at about the same time that the Sheriff's rescue helicopter found us. We were so relieved.

Getting Found

Our original Action plan had us getting to the parking lot no later than three o'clock in the afternoon. Some of the parents were supposed to meet us there to pick us up. When we didn't show up, and the hours kept ticking by, a worried parent called the Sheriff's Department, and a search and rescue team was dispatched. The helicopter arrived and dropped blankets for us and everything, but by then we were only about a mile from the parking lot. We weren't really cold either. We just wanted to go home and get off that trail.

I remember being so glad to be done. I hadn't really gotten injured, but other people had some minor cuts, sore muscles, big blisters, and cactus pokes. In the process of trying to find our way out, my scout leader had climbed some of the rises around us to try to get a better view of the lay of the land. During one of those extra hikes, he'd fallen and gotten pretty bruised and cut up, but he didn't mention it. He just felt bad that he'd taken us all so far off track and worried so many people. Ultimately, though, he got us back "safely." Things could have been so much worse than they were. We could have been stumbling through cacti or tripping over rocks. We could have all been cut up and bruised. Someone could have broken something; then we would have had to carry that person—making the hike that much more dangerous and exhausting.

In the end, the hike was so brutal that some of the boys never came back to scouts. They'd survived the hike, but they were so focused on the negative side of the pain, delirium, and misery that they couldn't bring themselves to ever face anything like it again. On the other hand, some of us were proud of what we'd done. Sure we'd experienced the same aches, pains, and misery, but we were through it now. We'd gained the Experience and no one could take that away from us.

And this is where that second tool comes in. You can have the exact same Experience as someone else, negative or positive, and come out of it with a totally different perspective than that other person. Which way you see it is largely influenced by your past Experiences, but you are still free to pick how you look back on it. Would I ever want to do that hike that way again? Of course not. Especially not at age 11. The hike was so bad that I actually lost my taste for hiking for a lot of years, but it didn't prevent me from sticking with Scouting and eventually achieving the rank of Eagle Scout. As a matter of fact, it made me feel as though I had earned my way to that prestigious rank. I learned from the experience to the point that today, if I were going to go the long way again, I'd go prepared. I would bring more food, more water, and a flashlight with spare batteries. I'd also mentally prepare myself better.

In a way, though, none of the difficulty matters because we *made* it. We *did* it. We were successful against the odds. After going through an Experience like that, why wouldn't you look back and accept it as the success that it was instead of focusing on the negative? Have you ever known someone to go through the most awful hardship yet come out as a better person? That's the crucible in action; that's refinement. Admittedly, some people go through hardship and get worn down by it, but those people generally aren't focused on a higher purpose. They are focused on the difficulty of the moment, not what they stand to gain after passing through the crucible.

This is where entering the crucible with the intent to exit comes in. We don't always choose to enter the crucible—for instance with health issues or going on a day hike that lasts well into the night—but we can always choose to turn our focus forward and look to the goal and what we stand to gain. Then, once we're through the Experience, we can look back on it and draw whatever lessons we choose to. Some people employ their confirmation bias to choose only the negative lessons—those are the scouts who never came back. They'd had a bad Experience and projected that Experience forward to the rest of their possible scouting activities. As a result, they decided to opt out.

Most of us, however, look back on that Experience with something akin to fondness—especially a few decades later. I wouldn't want to do it again, and I wouldn't want to put anyone else through it either, but I learned something about myself on that hike. I learned that I can push myself to go so much farther than I ever dreamed of. I was planning on pushing myself just to hit the 12-mile mark. To look back and find out we'd gone closer to 30 miles was amazing. If you'd have told me that morning that I was about to go do a 30 mile hike, I'd have told you that you were crazy. I never would have signed up to go that distance. To look back and find out that I could actually do it is a priceless lesson. We went two and a half times as far as we planned, yet we made it.

Silver Linings

How many boys that age get the chance to have that kind of Experience? Not many. The other boys who kept coming to scouts and I wanted to put it on a t-shirt or something else to memorialize it. We were so proud of ourselves after that. We had accomplished something that everyone would have told us was impossible—something we ourselves would have said was impossible. We'd hiked nearly 30 miles in a "single" day. Even most adults can't claim that kind of achievement. That Experience was a huge boost to our individual Confidence because we were able to look back on the good things that came out of it.

Sure we went the long way around and ended up lost and scared and everything else, but we were never really in any danger. In fact, once we realized we were lost, we stopped trying to find the shortest route to home; we just focused on taking the surest way—even if it ended up being another "long way." And that's another principle that I learned from this Experience. Sometimes, the goal is worthwhile but the process can leave you feeling lost. When that happens, it's sometimes better to just focus on a sure way to the goal rather than trying to find the fastest or easiest way. The important thing is to get there in one piece.

This Experience also shaped me in the sense that I wasn't afraid to try difficult things—or at least not as afraid. I know that I can head out into the wilderness with little more than a sketchy map and still find my way. I don't mean that in a literal, physical, walk-out-into-the-desert sense, but it certainly holds true in the more ambiguous realms of personal relationships, business, and more. If you'll exercise your Hope and Belief by Taking Action, the Experience will come and help to refine you and teach you about how to correct your path. You don't need to start out in the exact right direction; just start in the general direction and refine your course as you go. This is a huge part of why the scouting program is so successful at shaping the lives of boys. Not by giving them chances to get lost on hikes, but to give them experiences that build confidence, however it comes. This confidence gives boys a lot of what they need to face a multitude of future life experiences.

I know not everyone believes the way I do, but I feel like you can ascribe a certain amount of your course in life to the gentle guidance of a higher power. You can call that power whatever you want—the universe, your higher self, etc.—but you will be guided into things and guided through them as long as you remain open to that guidance. And that doesn't mean that God always puts us into good situations—sometimes He provides a chance to grow—but I believe that good can come from any situation He puts us in. The trick is looking through those Experiences and drawing out the good—and recognizing the situations we've put ourselves into due to ignorance of or resistance to that divine plan.

You don't need to believe in a spiritual dimension to life in order to see the positive points of even the hardest things or most circuitous paths—even if that positive is as simple as the commiseration and support you receive from others. You also don't need to believe in God to see that things can work themselves out for the best as long as you stay committed. I believe that's the hand of divine intervention, but you don't need to. The point is, if you will push forward and continue to Take Action, you'll continue to gain Experience that helps you to learn the right way to do things. The How will work itself out as you continue to push forward. You'll get to your own Second Water eventually. It's nice if you can follow the map, but you can follow the map incorrectly and still arrive—still gaining valuable Experience along the way.

So when you look back on things, don't focus on the hardships and setbacks. Look for those times when you broke through and made progress. Look for the times when you learned how to do something, even if you failed at it first. Failure is, in many respects, the path to learning and growth anyway. If everything worked out the first time you tried it, you'd never need to work at anything. You'd never learn that valuable skill. You'd never get stronger. As it turns out, setbacks and resistance really are a good thing—even if they don't feel like it when you are in the middle of them.

In a way, you can look at hardship as an exercise class for your character. When you go to the gym to work out, you go knowing that it's going to be hard (and usually not fun), but you go because you want the results of the workout—a fitter body. When you face challenges along the path to your goals, think of them like workout sessions that will make you strong enough to achieve your goal. They will be hard at the time, but you can get through them alive. And, once you do, the fading affect bias will help to blunt the memory of the negative Experience in favor of the positive one.

Brands of Experience

So remember that how you look back on your Experience is up to you. Any Experience can be seen in a positive light if you'll just make an effort to see it that way. Some Experiences will be harder to see positive things in than others, but your limbic brain is pulling for you to feel the good things, not the bad ones. So keep Taking Action and moving forward. Focus on the positive Experiences in order to strengthen your Hope and Belief, and you'll be able to make it through the crucible to your goal at the other end.

With that destination in mind, you want to gain your Experience as quickly as possible. If you can make the goal a primary focus in your life, then you'll be able to progress that much more quickly. If you can't make it a primary focus, you'll move more slowly. As long as you stay focused, though, you'll continue to Take Action, gain Experience, and move forward. One more thing that will help you is actually recognizing all the Experience you are gaining. As we've discussed before, the neocortex can only focus on so much at once. Because of that bandwidth issue, you may have Experiences that you don't fully realize or appreciate—thus limiting their effectiveness in propelling you along.

So, as you Take Action to seek Experience, you need to recognize that there are a number of different kinds of Experience you can cultivate. Each of the different types of Experience is equally valid, though some are easier to obtain than others, depending on your individual goal. In a way, you could say that each has a unique set of strengths and weaknesses. Really, those strengths and weaknesses revolve more around the ability of a given Experience to apply to a new situation in terms of the level of compatibility you'll see. There are seven main types of Experience: physical, mental, emotional, spiritual/metaphysical, vicarious, social, and placebo. Let's talk about each.

Physical

Physical Experience is one of the more easily identifiable types of Experience because it's hard to ignore. When you fall and skin your knee, you can't exactly decide to just turn off the pain. You can keep going in spite of the pain, but the physical indicator of the Experience will remain. Physical Experience isn't always about feeling pain, however. Take marathoners as an example. These people push their bodies to the limit for weeks or even months in preparation for the ultimate event. They focus and train and watch what they eat—often without giving up anything out of their already busy lives.

When you look at the process for preparing for a marathon, you might be tempted to look at all the pain, sweat, and tears that a person could go through. Don't. Instead, focus on the evolution and growth that person is undergoing. Each time that person does another run and pushes a little further, he or she is getting a little fitter. That person is building a bit more endurance and strength. Each completed run is also an achieved subgoal in the greater, overall goal of running the marathon. Each time a person completes another run, he or she builds Experience and Confidence regarding the next run—and about overcoming any other obstacles life throws in the way. Running may not be easy, but it builds up a person with the knowledge that he or she can stick with something difficult and come out on top.

For this reason, physical Experience is a great way to build yourself up. When you set a challenging physical goal and then achieve that goal, you prove to yourself that you can do hard things. That Confidence will then spill over into other areas of your life, boosting your Hope and aggregate Belief in almost everything you do. On the other hand, setting a fitness goal and then giving up on it risks discouraging you in other parts of your life too.

Physical Experience doesn't necessarily come from only exercise either. You can participate in a hands-on lesson at work or school which is, at least in part, a physical Experience. Any time you engage your body in doing something, it becomes a physical Experience that you can later draw on to strengthen your Hope and Belief.

Mental

Mental Experience is the summation of the things that happen in your mind. They can occur in parallel with other Experiences, but they have a distinctly mental component. For instance, researchers are finding that physical exercise—when you focus on the exercise itself—actually has positive outcomes for the mind. In a way, working out your physical body also works out your mind—but only if you're paying attention. If you put on loud music or watch TV or a movie while you work out, you won't get the same benefit. The reason is simple: your mind isn't having the same Experience as your body. Your mind is somewhere else doing something else.

This is why people joke about being physically present but mentally absent—or about having no one home upstairs. This ability to disassociate your mind from your body is also the reason you can come home and sit on the couch after a brutal day at the office and not even remember the drive home—or the three hours of TV you just watched. If your mind gets tired enough, it can "go to bed" without your body, and the converse is also true. Ever had a night where you woke up at two in the morning with your mind racing? Your body was content to be totally limp and absent (still asleep), but your mind was feverishly dissecting a problem or situation. That's because your neocortex—your mind—is an entity unto itself. You can almost picture it like a tiny version of you walking around in your head throwing control levers for the rest of your brain and body. If that mini-you takes a break, your body doesn't necessarily suddenly collapse into a sleeping mess.

This break between mind and body presents you with a wonderful opportunity though. Because your body and mind don't always have to act together, you can do thought experiments. These were popularized by Einstein when he found that he didn't have the necessary technology to do the experiments he wanted to do. In the absence of the right equipment, he would just think about problems and carry them around to their possible outcomes. You can do the same. Having trouble with a coworker? Think through the situations and the different ways you could approach it. If you can be realistic about what's going to happen at each stage of the experiment, you can actually have an Experience that builds your Hope and Belief about going out and doing the real thing.

Emotional

Emotional experience is anything that you experience directly on an emotional level. That sounds obvious, but it's hard to identify experiences in life that are purely emotional because the limbic brain isn't under your conscious control. You choose to go out and do something physical because that's under your control. You can even do a thought experiment and exist solely in your mind for a time. Your neocortex can fabricate a reality for you in order for you to have a visceral, realistic experience even though there's nothing real about it. Having a purely emotional Experience, however, is far more complicated. Emotions don't really exist on their own. Emotions are the reactions of the limbic brain to whatever else is going on around you.

Ironically, for all their abstract nature, emotional experiences can actually be the most powerful kind of Experience. This goes back to the limbic brain being the source of the real driving power behind your efforts to achieve anything. If you recall, the limbic brain is the figurative heart of the human soul. Your neocortex thinks in logic and your limbic brain thinks in emotion. Whenever something "touches your heart" you've had an emotional Experience. Frequently, these Experiences come as physical or mental Experiences with an added layer, the emotional layer, and when you have an emotional Experience, it will carry a huge amount of weight—whether good or bad. This is why emotional injuries to kids can bring such long-lasting effects. Those Experiences carry that negative weight for years and years—defying even the fading affect bias to an extent, though anything can be overcome with time. Thankfully, deep emotions run both ways, and an emotionally positive Experience can carry you on high for a lifetime. At the risk of seeming cliché, I would say that meeting and marrying my wife led me to multiple ongoing positive emotional Experiences that have greatly influenced the person I've become.

The key to positive emotional Experiences is to train yourself to see the positive. You can't have an emotional Experience without it being tied to some other kind of Experience (because you can't summon emotions on command), so the weight of that emotional response will depend a lot on how you interpret that other experience. If you have a tragic, physical accident, you can look at the pain and loss and let that trigger negative emotions inside you, crippling yourself, or you can look at the chance you have to prove yourself and all the outreach from others and let that fuel positive emotions within you. Whichever way you go is largely up to you—which is why emotional Experience can play so heavily for you rather than letting yourself be a victim and having emotion play against you.

Spiritual

This final major type of Experience may get a little pushback from some, but I'm going to talk about it anyway because it's a powerful part of many people's lives, including my own. Before I begin, let me just explain first that a "spiritual Experience" doesn't necessarily mean a divine visitation or anything like that—though that would probably qualify! Rather, I'm talking about those times when you have insight beyond your own ability or peace in the midst of chaos. You don't even have to believe in God to have a spiritual experience. I know atheists who still have spiritual Experiences. The only difference is that they don't ascribe them to any divine source. Still the human soul is transcendent enough all on its own. If, for any reason, the term "spiritual" makes you uncomfortable, you can think of these instead as metaphysical Experiences. Metaphysical means "philosophical" or "abstract" especially in the context of existence and the purpose thereof.

Spiritual or metaphysical Experiences are often deeply tied in with emotion. Spiritual Experience is kind of like a second form of communication to that primal intelligence in your limbic brain. The difference is that it often carries an overtone which resonates with your neocortex. In effect, you are having an Experience which resonates in both your heart *and* your mind. Spiritual Experiences often carry a sense of wonder—a deep feeling of connection and amazement coupled with an inability to comprehend the connection even while knowing that it's real and instructive. Because of their ability to influence both the mind and the heart, spiritual Experiences can be extremely powerful. Best of all, you can actually seek these kinds of Experiences just like physical or mental ones.

The easiest way is through meditation and seeking for your "inner voice." I and many others do this through prayer, but the key is to open yourself to your surroundings and let your heart and mind work together. Often, these Experiences can lead to intense feelings of peace and security—even in the face of turmoil and chaos. They can also lead you to new ideas and approaches that you never would have otherwise considered. And let me just point out that the danger isn't in having these kinds of Experiences or in listening to them. The danger is in ignoring them. When you receive inspiration on a spiritual or metaphysical level, you should act on it. Failure to act will cause you to numb yourself to these inspirational influences over time. The greatest people I have known always attribute their upward path to the powerful influence of spiritual Experiences—regardless of who or what they view as their higher power.

Vicarious

The next three categories of Experiences don't really stand on their own. We've talked about the different facets of existence already (physical, mental, emotional, and spiritual), and these next classifications really layer on top of those categories. For instance, you can have a social spiritual Experience. People do it every week in church. You can also have a vicarious physical Experience by watching someone else burn themselves on the stove and deciding to never follow suit. So keep that in mind as we discuss these three classifications. You can almost look at these as methods for obtaining the types of Experiences.

First let's discuss vicarious Experience. This is, in its simplest form, simply learning about someone else's experience and assuming that for yourself. You know people climb ladders, so you assume you can too. When you learn about the sciences in school, you are learning vicariously. You're not doing the experiments and earning the Experience firsthand. You're taking the word of a historian about what has happened and learning from those Experiences. As the third of six children in my family, I had the benefit of watching and learning from the Experiences of my older siblings. I learned many good things from them and followed in their footsteps in many ways, but I also had the luxury of learning from their mistakes. What the actual consequences of breaking rules in our home looked like and how my parents reacted to various situations. I'm not saying I was a model teenager by any stretch, or that they were bad examples, neither is true. I'm just saying that I had some guinea pigs ahead of me who, like it or not, taught me a lot of beneficial things by way of observation.

Vicarious Experiences come in all shapes and sizes, and they're really easy to get—almost everyone is willing to share "advice" based on the things they've been through. As with my siblings, my parents often offered up their own experiences for reference—especially the stories they told me about their own childhoods. In fact, vicarious Experiences are so easy to have that our lives are full of them. For example, why do people like to watch TV or movies? You guessed it. Vicarious Experience. When you watch the hero save the day, you can have a vicarious Experience on an emotional level (or mental, physical, or spiritual—though vicarious physical Experiences are far less common).

One of the main benefits fans of professional athletics get is the feeling of accomplishment that comes when their team wins. It's such a desirable vicarious Experience that every winning team attracts a whole new crop of fans on their way to a championship. This and fandom in general is a great example of how people want the thrill of the win without being on the playing field. You might even say that this is the main reason we love athletic contests and why professional athletics has become the massive business it is today.

A key thing to remember about vicarious Experience, however, is that it's one of the weaker forms. If you can learn from someone else's Experiences, that's great. Don't change and don't lose that ability. Unfortunately, for most of us, there comes a time when we doubt the Experiences of others. You see this tendency in teenagers. They want to throw out all the vicarious Experience they've gathered over the years—everything their parents or teachers have ever told them—and go find out for themselves. If you find yourself in a situation where a vicarious Experience isn't carrying enough weight for you, don't sit around debating it. Go do something about it. Go seek the Experience for yourself. Make it personal, deep, and lasting. Please note that I'm not recommending that you break laws or do immoral things to learn for yourself, though some people seem to crave learning this way. I urge you to save yourself the heartache these types of Experiences will cause, and just recognize that vicarious Experience can be an extremely valuable tool. While vicarious Experience doesn't usually carry the same weight as personal Experience, you can certainly gather a lot more of it a lot more quickly at a lot less risk to yourself. That means more time and energy to focus on gaining the Experience you really need in order to move forward.

Social

Social Experience is any Experience that involves other people in some way. It can be you with other people doing the same thing or you directly interacting with another person (or persons) in some way. This is the idea that you can have a performance review with your boss or a heart to heart with your best friend as a social Experience and also that you can go to the beach or to a movie with people as a social Experience. Again, you can have any of the four main categories as a social Experience. The emphasis here is that these things happen in a group setting with social interaction. Thus watching a movie with others isn't really a social Experience until you start talking about the movie afterward—unless you talk *during* the movie—in which case I hope you're watching it at home. The key is that there is interpersonal interaction of some kind.

Social Experience is, in that way, one part vicarious and one part personal. It's somewhere in between. These are things you Experience through your social circles at work, school, home, church, rotary club, gym, etc. If the term "social" isn't descriptive enough for you, you can think of them as "group" Experiences instead. These are things that don't happen to you solely on an individual level because they happen to you at the same time as they happen to other people, and you are all connected and sharing with one another during the Experience. The nice thing about social Experiences is that, as parts of both sides, they kind of bridge the gap between personal and vicarious Experience. With a personal Experience, you're on your own to face any consequences and figure out your way through any setbacks or difficulties. You can reach out to others, but everything really rests on you. This makes the Experience deeper and more lasting, but it can also leave you feeling lost or beaten down. With vicarious Experience, nothing rests on you. You're just watching everything unfold or learning about how it unfolded afterward. The advantage is that you can assimilate the key points without going through the pain, but it means that the Experience tends to be very weak.

Social Experience works to bridge that gap. On the one hand, you are an active participant, so the Experience will mean more and last longer. This is good for building the weight of your positive Experience. On the other hand, you're not alone in the Experience, so you have other people to help you through, give ideas, and keep one another motivated. How much weight the Experience carries depends on how active you are as a participant. One of the big drawbacks of social situations is that it's easy to be a silent participant. It takes no effort to sit and watch everyone else figure things out—though your Experience shifts to be more of a vicarious one at that point.

Another important note about both social and vicarious Experiences is that they don't carry the same weight (or even the same polarity) from one person to the next. Think back to my hiking expedition with my scout troop. We were all shaken by the Experience, but some of us looked back on it as a growing, learning, strengthening, enriching Experience and others looked back on it as a disaster that should never be risked again—to such a point that they opted out of future opportunities entirely. We had basically the same Experience out on that trail, so what made us all so different? The weight of your pre-existing Experience and your attitude will largely determine how you take a new experience, which means that everyone receives Experience differently. None of us has the exact same set of Experiences, after all, and none of us has the exact same personality or attitude either. I point this out in an effort to encourage you to be cautious about the expectations you put on others regarding what they gain from vicarious or social Experience. You don't know everything about that person, so you can't possible hope to predict what they will or won't gain.

One phenomenon worth mentioning is the unique way that the individuals involved in a social Experience can shape perception of that Experience over time. While my dad didn't love hiking 30 miles with a group of scared and tired 11-year-olds, as he has shared his positive perspective on the experience over time it has been a major influence in shaping my opinion of the ordeal. If my parents had both been outraged about the way things turned out, they easily could have negatively affected my perspective and what I took away, even though nothing about the Experience was any different than before. Never underestimate your ability to offer a positive perspective on a social Experience, not only for your benefit, but also for the benefit of everyone else involved.

Placebo

The last classification for Experience that we need to cover here is kind of a strange one because, in a way, it's gaining Experience without actually going through an Experience. We talked about how daydreaming or performing thought experiments can furnish you with real Experience that has nothing to do with reality—making it fake Experience in a way. Well, your imagination isn't the only way to gain "real" experience without exposing yourself to the full range of "real" consequences. Another type of Experience you can gain is called placebo.

In medicine, a placebo is something you give to patients or test subjects to make them think they're getting a real drug. For instance, when studying a new pain medicine, you will administer some subjects with the actual medication and others with a placebo. You can't just administer the drug to some and not others because the mind has a powerful ability to skew the results. Your test subjects would know whether or not they were getting the medication, and they would react accordingly. By giving a placebo (sometimes called a sugar pill), you can fool everyone into thinking they're getting the medicine—putting everyone back on a level playing field and eliminating that bias. In the same way, you can have an Experience that isn't really what you think it is, thus gaining the benefits of the Experience even though it's all in your mind.

This seems like magic or something, but really it's more like science. In fact, school is a perfect example of placebo-centered Experience. You may do a few hands-on experiments in your science courses and you'll be doing actual computations in math, but much of the work is still placebo. It's all the effort and fear without any of the real consequences. After all, what's the worst that can happen if you screw up in school? You fail and get held back a year (if schools even hold kids back anymore). What's the worst that can happen if you really foul up in the workplace? You can end up out of a job with lawsuits coming down on you. Yet the stress and panic of being late or deficient on a school assignment is no less real than that same stress at work, and by learning how to struggle and manage your time with school projects, you prepare yourself for those same things in the workforce.

The whole concept of placebo is getting people to Believe something "untrue" so that they'll do what they need to. Then, once they've proven their ability and gained the Experience and Confidence, you can reveal the "truth" to them so they can see how that Experience applies to their real lives. Let me give you two more examples, one from a kids' movie and one from everyone's childhood. First, think of that little feather that Dumbo carries when he learns to fly. He Believes that he can fly only because of the magic in that feather—it has nothing to do with his "wingspan." Every time he flies, it's another placebo Experience. He is doing the flying, but he thinks that the feather is the reason. When he loses the feather, he loses his Belief—until a situation requires him to save the day. Then all that Experience bubbles up and he makes the connection between placebo and reality, enabling him to fly without the feather.

Think that doesn't happen in real life? Let's look at the second example. Who taught you to ride a bike? Chances are, whoever it was would run alongside you and slightly behind, holding the seat of your bike to help you balance. You were riding at first as a placebo—not in any real danger of falling but with all the Belief that you were riding your bike. What happened after the fifth or sixth pass when you glanced back to see Mom or Dad and realized there was no one there? Did you fall? Or did you realize that you were riding that bike all on your own? It was no longer a placebo Experience, it was the real thing. That's when that person stepped forward and let you know that you'd been riding on your own the whole time. You were fully capable of riding that bike and just didn't know it yet. When you made the connection, you were then able to have the Experience, Belief, and Hope to try riding a few more times—leading you to Confidence and the ability to ride. And you never forget how to ride a bike, right? That's because Experience (and Confidence) gained never really go away. They're yours to keep forever.

Discernment

So, now you know the importance of Experience and you know how to gain it. You know how to recognize all the Experience you're already gaining, and you know how to look for specific types and classifications of Experience that will match up with your goal. There's just one last thing to understand before you go and build up to critical mass. You need to understand that these principles work in both directions. If you are gaining the wrong kind of Experience (or Experience of the wrong things), you will be preparing yourself for the wrong things—preparing yourself for potential failure on a grand scale.

We've all heard the expression "practice makes perfect." I struggle to accept that idea the way it's written. My problem is that if your practice is imperfect, how can you possibly expect it to make you perfect? For instance, if you go to work out but do the exercises wrong, they won't have the intended effect. You'll get perfect at doing the exercises that way, but you won't be getting the results you're expecting—and you may actually be training yourself into a chronic injury. I'm more a fan of the phrase that "practice makes *permanent.*" When you practice something a certain way, you'll develop an affinity for doing it that way. Practice the wrong way and you won't be building your capacity to do something the right way.

That's why it's so critical for you to self-assess and reach out to mentors as you go. By taking a step back to review your actions and outcomes—especially if you can get someone else to help you look at it all—you can see whether you are doing the right actions and get back on track. In effect, this would be like adding GPS to that scout hike I took. We started on the wrong trail but had no way of knowing it until we were miles and miles in. In a way, we were doing the right thing by Taking Action and getting started, but we weren't on exactly the right path. If we'd had GPS, we could have referred to it to find out that we were steering off course much earlier on. It would have helped us to stay on track and would have shortened our journey considerably.

Now, if you can't find a mentor to help you see clearly, you can still make it through and be successful; it's just a lot harder to see the lay of the land when you're down in the trenches in the thick of the battle. A mentor can watch things from up above to help you see where to apply your efforts, but you can go ahead without one as long as you understand and are willing to accept that there will be extra effort involved. This is good because sometimes you can't find one. You can have anyone fill in as an accountability partner to help you keep pushing forward, but a mentor can give you that encouragement while also giving you more direction. Still, whether you can find a mentor or not, you should be able to do some soul searching and internal recalibration to keep you going in the right direction—at least generally speaking. To further that end, I'm going to talk to you about a few indicators you can use to determine whether your Experience is helping you or actually taking you off course.

Environment

First, what is the environment in which you're gaining this Experience? Is it a positive one? Does it align with who you want to become? In my late teens I was looking for summer employment to save money that I planned to use for college and volunteer missionary service—both important long-term goals to me. A good family friend was an upper manager for a large tire company and his office was at their main distribution center in downtown Phoenix, AZ about 45 minutes from where I lived at the time. He offered me a full-time job paying more than I could make anywhere else. So out of gratitude for the opportunity, respect for the friend, and probably a bit of desperation, I quickly accepted the position without doing any research.

I showed up my first day, eager to learn my duties, mostly just grateful to be working indoors. After I filled out the necessary paperwork, my manager led me out of his clean, air-conditioned office into the filthy, rubber-scented inferno they called a warehouse. It was June in Phoenix and the thermometer on the wall inside read 95 degrees Fahrenheit. I finally realized why there was a job opening and why the pay was better than other jobs I'd looked at! I immediately jumped in and learned the system for pulling tire orders by store and loading them on the right delivery trucks. By the end of that day I was tired, extremely dirty, and probably experiencing the beginning stages of heat stroke.

I came back the next day, the day after that, and every day the rest of the summer. I didn't miss a day of work, putting in all my scheduled hours and enduring the demanding work conditions. While I quickly surpassed my manager's expectations (I even got promoted to driving the delivery trucks on the afternoon shifts), none of the accolades meant anything to me. I had already made up my mind within the first few days that I was never going to do a job like this again. But not being much of a quitter, I stuck it out and excelled where I could, even though I can't think of a job I have liked less.

Looking back, it wasn't the job duties or the draining heat that were the most difficult. It was hard because I was locked into an environment where the Experience I was gaining was not what I wanted in life and didn't align with my Core Why. I learned a lot that summer, but the biggest takeaway was that while I could do anything I committed to, I would never put myself in another environment that didn't provide the Experience that I needed to progress toward my goals.

The same can happen to anyone anywhere if that person isn't careful about choosing his or her environment. Luckily, my unfortunate summer job resulted in mostly just physical discomfort and a bit of mental distress trying to stay committed while making the most of things. Other situations in your life may come along bearing far worse personal ramifications, exposing you to physical, emotional, moral, or spiritual dangers. So, briefly stated, if you want positive, uplifting progress in your life, make sure you're seeking it from positive uplifting environments where you can thrive. Let's break down environments into different parts.

Places

As a subset of environment, you can look specifically at the places where you go. What are they like? Are you spending time in cheap bars hoping to find Mr. or Mrs. Right? What are the chances that your lord or lady in shining armor is going to be in a place like that? If you want to be fit and trim, do you spend your time at the gym or in fast food restaurants? Do you see where I'm going with this? Your environment is the summation of several different components, and one of the most telling is the actual location.

Situations

Another subset of your environment is the kinds of situations you put yourself into. If you want to stop gossiping, for instance, you probably should avoid situations where the people around you are gossiping. If you find yourself in that kind of situation, leave, if not physically, at least mentally. It won't be easy, necessarily, but staying won't take you any closer to your goals. If you know you have temper issues and want to get better, try to avoid or defuse situations that would make you blow up. When people start getting in your face, warn them about what's coming and try to get away. If you are an addict, your first line of defense is to stay away from situations that will trigger or enable your addiction. You want to seek situations that will build you up and bring the right Experience for your goals.

Opportunities

Another thing to look at is the types of opportunities you're seeking. If you want certain kinds or levels of Experience in something, you need to be seeking opportunities that will give you that kind of Experience. It sounds simple, but we often get pulled into projects that don't serve our deepest needs. For example, if your goal is to influence thousands of people through writing and public speaking, you probably won't gain what you need working in a tire warehouse. If you know that getting the next big promotion at work requires you to have a certain skill level with spreadsheets and databases, you need to look for opportunities to develop that Experience and skills. That big sales convention might sound like a lot of fun and a great learning opportunity, but it's probably not going to teach you more about spreadsheets and databases, so you should most likely opt out in favor of what will get you to your end goal.

Potential

On the flip side of opportunities, you can look at things in light of what they *could* bring to you. When you need the opportunity to develop a specific skill, seek that opportunity. If another opportunity presents itself (like the sales convention I just mentioned), you need to weigh it out and see how it lines up with your objectives. Just because something sounds fun or sounds like a great chance to gain valuable Experience doesn't mean it's the right time for you to do that thing.

Instead, see if the Experience you expect to gain aligns with any of your goals. If not, put the opportunity on hold and focus on what will get you to where you want to go right now. However, I'm also proof that what you're looking for doesn't always come in the box you were expecting to have delivered. At the beginning of my high school career, I wasn't the vocalist my choir director was hoping for, but I was able to meet and far surpass his criteria over a short time. So while it's important to prioritize opportunities as they come, be sure you don't overlook the potential in some as they may more closely align with your Why and be exactly what you've been waiting for.

Summary

Personally, I find this function of discernment to be one of the roles of religion. No matter what religion you look at, the idea is to take people and give them a set of standards to guide their actions. While some find it terribly limiting, others, like me, find it freeing. I have benefitted greatly from finding a faith I believe in wholeheartedly. I have learned to make decisions long before I'm ever faced with the hard choice in the moment. I attribute much of my ongoing success in life to holding tightly to this set of moral standards. Metaphysics and divine inspiration aside, that's the point of any real religion—the push to help people be better today than they were yesterday and better tomorrow than they are today. If you feel like you need help making sure that your environment, situations, and opportunities are going to take you in a positive direction, consider getting more involved in religion. Accepted by the masses or not, it can help you to seek Experiences that will enrich you rather than leading you subtly downhill.

Whatever way you choose to manage your Experience portfolio is up to you. The most important thing for you to remember is that you will be gaining Experience every day whether you plan for it or not. You can choose to seek out uplifting Experience or you can default to whatever life throws your way, you will accumulate Experience either way. If you want to become the most that you can, you need to make sure you're taking charge of how those Experiences come to you and how you react to them. Life will still throw you curve balls no matter how careful you are, but knowing that they're coming (even if you don't know exactly when) can help you prepare to take them the way they should be taken—in stride. Remember, your objective is to build up a critical mass of positive Experience in order to propel yourself forward and reach for success. Once you reach that threshold, you will be unstoppable in your pursuit of the ultimate goal. You'll be well on your way to victory.

MOMENTUM

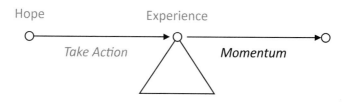

Momentum - [moh-men-tuh m]
- n. - force or speed of movement; impetus, as of a physical object or course of events[8]

What is Momentum? Momentum, as defined in physics, is equal to the product of mass x velocity. In layman's terms, you can think of it as a force equal to the weight of an object multiplied by how fast it's going. You can also think of it in terms of a freight train or avalanche. Does that sound pretty unstoppable? It takes miles of hard braking to stop a train, and nothing really can stop an avalanche. Momentum is a force to be reckoned with, and it can be *your* force to be reckoned with.

p=m*v

In physics, p is the symbol for momentum (probably because m and M are already taken for other things). If you want, you can think of it as p for *push* because your Momentum is like the sum of

<hr>

[8] momentum. Dictionary.com.*Dictionary.com Unabridged.* Random House, Inc. http://dictionary.reference.com/browse/momentum (accessed: February 18, 2015).

all your pushing, and it works to push you forward now. The equation for calculating Momentum is p=m*v, or p=mass*velocity. We already know that velocity is your Hope. It's what gives you both speed and, paired with a What, direction. As you increase your Hope, you build up your Momentum. But what is the mass in this equation?

On the one hand, the mass signifies the amount of Experience you've accumulated. As you Take Action and gain Experience, you build toward that critical mass. But it's more than that too. Saying that mass is simply Experience glosses over the details and inhibits your ability to focus on building mass. Mass *is* Experience, but it's really comprised of the things that bring Experience. Specifically, mass is comprised of the energy, commitment, sacrifice, and time that go into building Experience. Why do you care about targeting specifics and building mass? Because your amount of mass affects your long-term commitment to your goal. No matter how powerful your Hope is, velocity will only get you so far. The real key to success is to leverage your Hope into Taking Action and building Experience. That's what will carry forward. You can look at it as the comparison between an arrow and a boulder. The arrow has so much velocity that you can't even see it until it arrives, but an arrow doesn't have the force (the Momentum) to punch through a bale of hay. A boulder, on the other hand, has an insane amount of mass. It won't be easy to get that boulder moving, but once it starts, it can blast through a building—let alone a bale of hay—and it'll be traveling slow enough for you to see it the whole time. So let's take a look at how you can focus on building your mass.

Energy

Energy is, of course the level of effort you're willing to put into your goal, but it's also a measure of how your goal makes you feel. A goal that inspires you will unlock more energy within you than a goal that you feel less passionate about—that's another reason why it's so critical to start by finding your Why. The other aspect of energy deserves a little more coverage though. Energy, or effort, comes in all the same varieties as Experience (physical, mental, emotional, and spiritual). The kind of energy you put into an Action generally indicates the kind of Experience you'll get out, but not always. In a way, you can think of your goal like a battery; it needs a certain amount of energy to be fully charged—at which point that Confidence will power you into your next endeavor.

Commitment

Next is commitment. This is kind of an interesting precursor to Experience because your level of commitment is also influenced by your Experience. Because of that relationship, an increase in commitment can cause you to build your Experience and Momentum more quickly, but a decrease in commitment can also work against you. The way you see this happen most often is that a person will try something and have a bad Experience which shakes his or her Belief and commitment to the cause, and because they are less committed they start to have less Experience than they were having before. This vicious cycle robs many of us of our dreams, and it all can be traced back to our original commitment. In a way, commitment works as a kind of filter when we view our Experiences and look for relevant connections. If you are committed, your confirmation bias will be working in your favor. If you aren't committed, your confirmation bias will be working toward whatever else you're focused on.

Sacrifice

Third is sacrifice. Sacrifice is the act of giving up something you value for something you value even more. For example, if you ever give blood, you value the ideal of saving lives more than having unbroken skin and full veins. Granted, the needle poke will heal and your body will regenerate the blood, but you're still giving up a piece of yourself in hopes of saving someone else. The only catch to this is that you have to be giving up something you value. It doesn't really mean anything to you to give away something you don't care about. It's only when you give up something you would have liked to keep that you are able to roll those feelings over to your greater desire. In a way, the act of sacrificing allows you to aggregate your commitment and energy to make them count for more.

The other important role of sacrifice is that it ties you to your cause. Consider the level of commitment and love that a mother feels for her newborn child. While men experience powerful feelings in this setting, they are far surpassed by the mother who has carried the child through sickness, discomfort, sleeplessness, and other kinds of sacrifices for nine months. One could argue that this is a God-endowed process that endears mother to child across all of creation. No doubt sacrifice has a powerful effect on our Momentum.

Time

Last of all, time is the ultimate agent for building the mass of your Momentum. The reason is simply that more time gives you the space and recovery to expend more effort. The relationship is really that simple. The more time you spend focused on your goal, Taking Action, and moving forward, the more time you will be spending to build up that precious weight of Experience. If you can put forth a lot of effort, you can accumulate that Experience at a more rapid rate. But time is the great equalizer. No one has more or less in a day or week than anyone else. Harness this aspect of gaining Experience by not giving up just because you've been at something for a long time with seemingly few results. It's very likely that you're just on the verge of breaking through. As long as the goal is still worthwhile, there's no reason to quit working toward it. Time is your friend.

Tipping the Scales

When I was originally developing The Belief Blueprint, I was struggling with what image to use to represent it, and one of the biggest reasons I was struggling was because I wanted to find something that could represent this concept of Momentum. Initially, I considered several different models; we'll even talk about the very first version toward the end of the book. But it's instructive right now to look at one of the pieces that I really like but ultimately couldn't fit in the final model—a set of scales—something I call The Scales of Experience.

I liked the idea of scales because I really liked how it showed the visual of positive Experience tipping toward Momentum. Momentum is this idea that you start small and slowly build up until you have something unstoppable. This could be a business you start in your garage, a relationship, a skill that begins as a hobby, or anything else. Momentum is what you build over time as you grow and expand your positive Experiences. As your Hope and Belief drive you to Take Action, you'll gain Experience. We've already talked about how there will come a point when positive Experience reaches a "critical mass" of sorts. Critical mass is another physics term and refers to the amount of a radioactive substance you need for it to begin a chain reaction and explode—becoming a nuclear bomb. In other words, once you collect enough of the material together, it will start to react all on its own, driving to an explosive conclusion.

Experience works the same way in terms of reaching your success— except without the exploding part. You build and build your level of Experience through the things we just talked about until you reach a point where it all comes together and things start to flow. That doesn't mean that it takes any less Action or effort to move forward, but it will still feel easier at the same time. Let me put it to you this way. Have you ever tried something that was really hard at first but, over time, became easier and easier until it almost felt like you could do it in your sleep? Or like the task would almost complete itself? You were seeing firsthand the effect of Momentum. It wasn't that what you were doing somehow changed to be simpler; it's that your level of Experience made you a veteran of the process. In the words of Ralph Waldo Emerson, "That which we persist in doing becomes easier for us to do;

not that the nature of the thing itself is changed, but that our power to do is increased."

The idea behind the scales is that you would pile all your Hope, Belief, and positive Experience on one side to counterbalance all your Doubt and negative Experience on the other side. Initially, the scales would be tipped low because of your uncertainty and lack of Experience. As you Take Action, you start piling Experience on the other side until the scales tip in your favor. At that point, you reach that critical mass of Experience so that Momentum begins working for you. Ultimately, I decided that the scales weren't a good representation because they don't reflect the movement you make as you shift from Hope to Confidence. I wanted something that showed the relationship of the scales yet also left room to show the movement you make from one side to the other. That's where the seesaw came in.

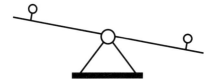

The seesaw has the virtue of tipping over just like a set of scales when you cross from the one side to the other. Even better, the seesaw shows the relationship of what happens as you move from left to right. Specifically, as you reach that critical mass of Experience at the fulcrum point, what will happen to the seesaw? That's right. It'll start to tip. As you reach and cross that threshold, your Hope will be elevated, rising up and lowering the height of the Confidence point. As you continue to Take Action, that Confidence point will drop until, rather than looking way up high and out of reach, it'll be on the ground, ready for you to take it. There is, of course, the unfortunate nature of seesaws in that they go up and down over and over, but we'll cover why that doesn't happen in the next chapter when we talk about Confidence. For now, just know that the seesaw really only goes one way. The model is complete when you reach the point of Confidence.

Downhill Side

The beauty of being able to tip the seesaw is that it shows the most important aspect of Momentum—you get to move downhill. When you initially sit on the seesaw, the whole thing is uphill. It's a steady rise from where you start to where you want to end. That can be very intimidating. As you gain Experience, however, you learn the ins and outs of your particular goal. You learn about how to work the system and how to leverage your efforts to put them where they'll count the most. In addition to learning about your goal, you'll be learning about the process of getting to your goal. Both kinds of knowledge will help you to move more quickly. It won't take any less effort, necessarily, but you'll spend less and less time wandering off on the wrong trail and more time heading straight for Second Water—straight for your goal.

In a way, this will make it feel like you're taking less effort, but the truth is you're just *wasting* less. Once you have enough Experience, you'll tip to the other side, and the rest of the journey will be downhill. Now it's Confidence that seems close and easy to attain while looking backward at the time when all you had was Hope seems far away and hard to comprehend. Of course, you still have to put one foot in front of the other and Take Action, but it should feel easier now. In addition to knowing what you're doing, you've built up all that ability through the Actions you've already taken. There are two important things to note here though. First, a common mistake that people make is thinking that tipping the model is the same thing as reaching the goal. It isn't. Second, when you're at that critical mass level, there's still a chance you could tip back the wrong way once or even multiple times.

Side, Not Slide

It's important to recognize that being on the downhill *side* of the model isn't the same as being on a downhill *slide*. There is a certain temptation as things start to make sense to throttle back and check the goal as completed. It isn't. Look at the model again.

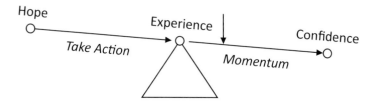

As you can see, the goal is clear down at the Confidence end. If we were in a mall, that indicator just to the right of the pivot point would say "You Are Here." Your Experience has reaffirmed your Hope and Belief, boosting you up the slope and past the middle, but making the seesaw tip isn't the goal. Reaching Momentum isn't the goal. Reaching Confidence—your What—is the goal. If you quit just past the fulcrum, you haven't quite made the goal yet. You've just figured out a lot about How to reach the goal.

This is a common mistake people make. The moment they start to see results and everything starts to come together, they check the box and move on without cementing the results. They've built up enough valuable Experience to understand what's going on, so they figure it's time for a new challenge and they stop working. The problem is that they haven't actually developed mastery yet. They're only operating on Experience, so at most they can be called experts—and we all know how often experts still get things wrong. The issue is that reaching Momentum doesn't mean you've built enough Experience behind you to really fully understand all the details about what you're doing. There's still some trial and error left in the system. Momentum just signifies that you've reached the point where your trials and errors are fewer and farther between. There's nothing that says you've completed the journey yet.

Even when people do realize that they need to keep seeking more Experience, they somehow feel like reaching the Momentum side means they can slide down the rest of the way without real effort. They think they can coast and let that Momentum carry them. This is the tempting allure of mediocrity, or the satisfaction of being "good enough." Think of a car on the highway. If you take your foot off the gas, what happens to your speed? It starts to slow down, doesn't it. This even happens when you go downhill much of the time. You can crest the hill and relax your foot on the accelerator, but you can't take your foot off entirely. You have to keep the engine engaged or it will actually act as a brake and slow you down. Big trucks have what are called "engine brakes" which basically force the engine to throttle down and slow by adding resistance to the exhaust flow—putting pressure on the rest of the drive system to slow down too.

In fact, you can do this to yourself too. Momentum can be bled away by braking yourself. Momentum should make it easier to push forward by making your efforts more efficient and effective, but if you choose to stop putting in any effort, you are choosing to stall out. Once you make that choice, you'll end up frozen in place on the downhill slope to success. To an extent, you're immune to Doubt because you already know too much. You know you can make it if you want to. You've evolved past simple Belief. Knowledge can't be shaken so easily. However, Hope is still an emotional thing, and "Inspiration without Expression is [still] Depression." If you stall out on the home stretch, you can still end up in Despair, but it'll be for different reasons. No one can take your Experiences from you, but you can choose to shelve them in the back recesses of your mind and ignore them. If you do, you won't make your goal. The only good news is that you've at least already tipped the scales. You might not be on your way to the finish anymore, but you're not going to slide backward either. If you ever come back to the goal, you'll find your readiness at basically the same level where you left it. The same can't be said of people who turn off before starting down the hill.

Don't Backslide

The reason I point this out is because that fulcrum point is critical in your progress. It's the final time when you can still tip and fall backwards into Doubt and Despair. Once you cross over the fulcrum and start to feel Momentum, you can put the brakes on and halt in your progress, but you'll never give up the Experience you have and that feeling that you're on the downhill side. You may choose to never make it to your goal, but the seesaw is already tipped and that won't change. When you're at the fulcrum shifting into Momentum, however, you can still stumble and fall backward, tipping the seesaw the wrong direction again and setting yourself up to start over.

To picture this happening and how it might feel, consider that you got a new job a few months ago. You've been working hard to learn everything you need to, and you're finally to a point where you don't need your boss to double check everything you do. You're feeling good about yourself, and you Believe that you can really have everything down before long. Initially, you felt like you were swamped and running around all the time. Now you've got your systems in place to keep you on track and on top of the game. Then your boss walks in one morning and fires you. She tells you that you're just not getting it—even though it's been more than a week since she last had to make you redo something. On your way to work that morning, you were feeling pretty sure of yourself. Now how are you feeling?

That experience could totally wipe a person out. Once you've reached Momentum, you are typically moving forward quickly enough to shrug off negative remarks. Just prior to that point, however, you are still vulnerable—perhaps more vulnerable than at any other time. If your boss had come to you three weeks before—when you were still getting help—and told you that you weren't getting it, you might have just agreed and walked away. You *weren't* really getting it yet. Not all the way, anyway. But once you hit that balance point where your Hope and the Goal are on the same level, you can tumble backwards just like you can move forwards. All it takes is the wrong kind of push at the wrong time with you not ready—especially if you've basically decided to stand still for a while. It's not all that dissimilar from trying to balance on the center point of a real seesaw. It's not stable. You might be able to pause for a breath on the upward climb or on the downward side, but trying to pause in the middle is a recipe for disaster—and keep in mind that I don't advise pausing either. There's too much risk when you try to stand still. The only safe course is to continue to Take Action—and that means moving your feet.

Making Your Experience Work

Gaining Experience without allowing yourself to move your feet in the right direction is kind of like building a fire but never using a match to light it. That stack of logs will look great there in the hearth, but it's not going to help anyone. In the same way, you can amass a huge amount of Experience without ever having it help you. I know that seems to be contrary to some of what I've said, so allow me to clarify. The value of Experience is when it plays in to give you Momentum, when it helps you move your feet. If you have a great experience but do nothing with it—you fail to change or grow from it—then you've basically just filed it away as being worthless. The value in Experience is the value of moving forward and Taking Action. It's the value of slowly changing your whole paradigm. Let your Experience change you for the better. That's what brings you to this point of Momentum. If you just shelve that Experience, you may as well have not wasted your time in earning it.

When you first start out after choosing a goal, you are Hopeful but uncertain. Your past completed Belief Blueprints have led you to Believe you can do it, sparking your Hope, but you're still carrying plenty of Doubt because this is a new situation. That Doubt can be very persuasive—especially if you listen to it. Each Experience you have should help to refine you and shed that Doubt. It should replace the Doubt with more Hope and increased Belief, but it can only do that if you act on it. You have to allow that Experience to change you and make you grow. If you do, you'll be building Momentum. If you don't, you'll quickly feel like you're just wasting your time. Instead of replacing your Doubts with positive Experience to build Belief, you'll be straining to carry the whole load all the time. You can only reach the point of Momentum when the sum of your efforts and positive Experiences exceeds the resistance of your Doubts. That's what tips the teeter-totter.

Because of that relationship, if you try out something new and totally knock it out of the park a few times, the weight of that Experience can be enough to tip the scales all on its own and put you straight into the Momentum phase. That doesn't happen very often, but it does happen. Usually, people look at it as tapping into their natural talent, and the results can be very gratifying. Alternatively, what seems to happen far more often, you can suffer what feels like a never-ending series of setbacks and move very slowly. The good news is that whichever happens is somewhat irrelevant. By building up your reserve of Experience and then leveraging it to work for you, you can accelerate yourself into the Momentum phase. As you've already learned, there are all kinds of Experience out there, and much of what feels like negative Experience at the time can actually work out for your benefit. Moving backwards isn't necessarily a bad thing if you observe it in the right way.

Bow and Arrow

After all, simply moving your feet may not always give you the result you expected right away. If you keep moving, you *will* get there eventually, but Taking Action doesn't *always* mean moving forward. This is one of the reasons why the Momentum stage of the Belief Blueprint is so refreshing. Once you reach the Momentum stage, you'll finally be moving forward nearly all the time. Do you remember back at the very beginning when we talked about society's view of success being this Point-A-to-Point-B straight line? Do you remember how I told you that society's perception is wrong? The real path to accomplishment is more like a tangled squiggle. The reason Momentum feels like smooth sailing is because you've done most of the squiggling already, or at least learned to anticipate the turns in the road better. You could also compare it to the feeling you get hitting pavement after driving on a dirt road for a long time. The journey isn't over, the road just got smoother.

Maybe the most difficult thing about working toward an objective is narrowing down that objective to its core existence and then figuring out the best way to get there. That takes a lot of effort—sometimes repeated effort. Sometimes it even requires you to step back now and then to get your bearings again. That's why we talked about mentors as such a helpful thing.

Some people get really discouraged by all that backtracking and backward movement. They look at it as a waste of effort and time. Sometimes, in going backward and forward and backward again, they get so discouraged that their Hope fades into Despair. This is a common thing, and it's a shame because it's all based on an incorrect view of how you get from Hoping to having something and then to being Confident in that thing. The truth is, going backwards is sometimes an integral part of the learning process. Instead of thinking like a sprinter, you need to think more like an archer.

How far could you shoot an arrow if you put it on the bowstring and never pulled? The arrow would just fall off at your feet, right? Well, you aren't the archer in this popular example. You're the arrow. If you never went backward, you'd never build up that pressure and energy to launch forward. The further back you go (the more Experience you obtain), the faster your speed will be once you reach that pivot point and launch forward into Momentum. So if the squiggle doesn't feel right for you, think of your journey like that of an arrow. You'll spend some time pulling backward before you can fly forward to your target. The more Experience you build up, and the clearer you are about your Core Why and your final goal, the stronger your Momentum will be. You can also think about this with respect to a gun. The hammer has to move back before it can slam forward and send the bullet into the bull's-eye. Even drag racers usually slide sideways before their tires grip and launch them up the track.

So don't worry about all that time you spent wandering back and forth across the actual path. If you've ever seen a dog on a long walk, you'll have a visual of how this process works. Initially, the dog runs all over the place—forward, backward, and side to side—always staying within a certain range of its owner. As the walk progresses, however, the dog will limit its free ranging until it's basically just walking beside the owner the whole way. In spite of all that bounding around, the dog is always making the same forward progress as the owner, it's just expending more effort initially. Later on, it catches on and falls in line, making its efforts far more efficient. By the end of the walk, both dog and owner arrive home together. Just like my scout troop, the dog has gone much farther than strictly necessary, but it still got to the end destination because it kept moving its feet.

Instead of feeling like you're losing ground, consider that to be the time when you're priming the arrow. You're pulling back the string and getting ready to fly. That way, when you do launch, you won't be surprised or alarmed by it. It will just be confirmation of what you already knew was coming, and the Momentum you've built up through your committed effort and sacrifice over time will lift you and push you forward. With that said, Momentum is kind of a hard concept to explain in technical terms but a very easy concept to show with examples, so I'd like to give you a couple examples now so that you can see how Momentum works in real life. Then we'll finish up by talking about what it really means to you.

Life's Like a Train

Did you know that freight trains move backward intentionally before starting off? If a freight train tried to start out by pulling the whole load at once, it would end up spinning its wheels. Steel wheels on steel rails don't produce much friction, and that's by design (it reduces fuel costs for a train under a heavy load). Without traction (and probably even with traction), a train engine can't simply muscle the whole train into movement. Instead, it has to start smart. So it'll back up and push the front cars toward the back ones. There's some play in the connection arms that attach the cars together, so this play allows for some compression in the overall length of the train. Then, when it's time to go, the engine will start forward pulling only its own weight. In a moment, it'll reach the limit of the connection to the first car and start pulling that too. A moment later, the engine will start pulling the second car—but it won't be doing it alone. Instead, the weight (actually the *Momentum*) of the first car will combine with the Momentum and pulling power of the engine to tug the second car into motion. The same thing happens with the third car and so on. Each car is pulled to life by the combined Momentum of the engine and all the other cars in front of the one getting started. In this way, a train engine is able to start pulling huge loads—because it lifts each segment individually. It could never do that if it didn't go backwards first.

Once that engine manages to get everything moving, something magical happens. The engine couldn't pull everything from a stop at the same time, but it has enough power to accelerate everything once it's started. It's a slow process to get tens of thousands of tons of materials moving, but speed builds up as the engine keeps investing energy and effort. Then, at some point, the train reaches the maximum safe speed for the tracks and the engine can relax a little, or at least, the load will seem lighter even if the engine is still pulling at full strength. That's why this compares so nicely to you on your path toward your goal. The biggest difference is that you won't jump the tracks by going too quickly, so you don't ever need to throttle back. And there's another difference related to the load you're carrying.

Be the Engineer

That freight train is carrying all kinds of supplies, cargo, and other materials. Those things need to get to an end destination. The things you're carrying *don't* need to make it to the end destination. Also, where a train needs to stop in order to drop off cars along the way, you don't. In fact, the more cars you drop, the more you can focus your efforts on gaining speed and leveraging your Momentum to make you unstoppable. Here's how it works. As you build up positive Experience, you can disprove your Doubts and erase them permanently. Each time you crush another Doubt, you lose another heavy car off the back end of the train. No stopping or detouring; you just drop it right off the side of the tracks. This is another benefit of building Momentum— decreased fear and Doubt. Momentum comes by both increasing your positive force and decreasing your negative force, or resistance. All the Doubts and concerns you had when you started will melt away at an ever-increasing pace as you build Momentum, allowing you to drive yourself to new record speeds.

And, if you think about the power and speed of a freight train, it's almost frightening in its unstoppability. There's a reason that Superman is compared to a locomotive. The front end of a train is armored like a tank because anything it hits will be obliterated. They put cattle guards on early trains to make sure that livestock didn't get smashed apart and pulled under the wheels. Once you've got Momentum on your side, you can smash right through your obstacles. Remember Momentum is mass times velocity. A freight train has a huge amount of mass, and it can travel fast enough to outrun you on the freeway (though they often don't for safety concerns).

The point is, you are just like that freight train when you start out.

It might feel impossibly hard to get traction at first, but the harder the struggle during the beginning, the harder you'll be going at the end because you'll have replaced that much more Doubt with positive Experience. Just remember that your Doubts are really invitations to become something even stronger.

Spinning Flywheels

This is similar to the concept of the flywheel. A flywheel is a large, heavy wheel generally attached to some form of machinery. The wheel is so heavy that it's extremely hard to turn at first. In fact, you might not be able to get it started at all without help. The first rotation can actually seem almost impossibly hard. Then, with each subsequent rotation, it will feel easier and easier to turn. You'll still be straining with all your effort to turn it, but you'll be getting better and better results as you go. As you continue to put in energy, you'll be building up all that energy for a time when you need to release it all at once—greatly exceeding your output for any given moment.

The advantage of a flywheel is that it can store up a lot of kinetic energy (the energy of movement). This can then be used in two basic ways. First, that energy can be used when the machine hits resistance of some kind. The flywheel will transfer that stored energy, and power through the resistance. This is especially useful in manufacturing industries, but the analogy is useful everywhere. By pushing hard now and storing up that energy, you can be banking it for the time when an obstacle might arise that, otherwise, you wouldn't have the strength to overcome. By building that Momentum, you'll be able to overcome that otherwise-impossible challenge. Second, flywheels work to smooth out irregularities in effort over time. When you put extra effort in, the flywheel will store that extra. When you have a time that you come up a little short, the flywheel will supply the extra. This gives you a much smoother plot of effort over time, helping you to avoid burnout while also helping you to avoid giving up at just the wrong time (right before you start to really get to the results and rewards of your efforts).

Each time you set a new goal, it's as if you're installing a new flywheel in your life. Each time you install a new flywheel, you have to put in time and effort to get it spinning. You have the energy of all your previous successes (your old flywheels; past successes) to help you jumpstart the new wheel, but you're still going to have to put in a lot of effort. As you get the wheel going, however, your efforts will yield more and more visible results. You'll bank up that energy and be ready to release it when you hit those tough times, pounding through and carrying forward. Can you see the similarities to the freight train here?

How This Matters

Your goals, aspirations, dreams, and intentions are all like the freight train or the flywheel. Each machine requires effort to get it started and effort to keep it going. Also like these examples, your efforts will bring you increasing results over time. You'll see and feel the difference slowly as you progress, but the change will still be there. The key points to remember are (a) that the hardest part is always at the beginning, (b) the difficulty will fade over time, and (c) you'll never be able to stop giving effort.

The beautiful part of the process is that, as you move along, your entire view of the world will change. Initially, you'll be living with your Doubts and fears. Then, as you build Momentum, you will actually start to see your own power for shaping your future. You'll be shedding those cars of Doubt and getting your flywheel up to speed. Your expectation of being able to then further shift your future will also change. You'll realize that you have the power to become something much greater than what you've been in the past. More importantly, you'll be moving beyond those initial Doubts and seeing your current goal in a new light. Instead of just Hoping and Believing that you can reach it, you'll start to Know you can reach it. That Knowledge is the final stage of the Belief Blueprint, and we'll cover it in detail in the next chapter. First, there's one last aspect of Momentum that we need to cover in order to help you leverage the concept to its fullest. It has to do with setting the proper expectations for yourself as you start off on any new venture.

10,000 Hours

Time and time again, I've seen people start toward a worthy goal but then quit right before the end. For a time, I assumed it was because they got bored or were just too lazy. As I've grown and learned, I've come to realize that I was wrong—at least in the case of most people. Most people don't quit because they're lazy or bored or anything like that. Instead, my experience is that most people quit because they get discouraged that things take longer than they expect. We've already talked about this phenomenon before when we talked about goals. At that point, I warned you to not expect an overnight turnaround. That warning still holds true, but let's look a little more closely about how long you *should* expect.

The truth is that modern research actually gives us a window into just how long it can take to develop a new skill or improve yourself. The prevailing theory today indicates that about 10,000 hours of steady, effective practice can bring you to a "mastery" level for just about anything (the actual numbers vary between around 8,000 up to about 12,000 depending on the skill; 10,000 is just a nice round number in the middle). Now, not all things are complex enough to need that kind of time commitment, but it puts things into perspective nicely. Let's break it down for just a moment. If you work 40 hours a week for 50 weeks a year (we'll give you 2 weeks' vacation), you'll be putting in 2,000 hours. That means that you can master something in a mere 5 years if you make it your full time job. Sound daunting? You should keep in mind that not everything in life will take 10,000 hours to learn. For instance, you can learn to play piano in less time than that. After just a few years of lessons and consistent practice, you can be at a level where you can play most common pieces with reasonable proficiency. Getting in shape also takes less than 10,000 hours. The more ordinary a goal seems, the more likely that it will take fewer than 10,000 hours.

This 10,000 hour target is for complex skills in which you want *mastery*, not just proficiency, so don't get discouraged that everything is going to take five years of full-time work. Proficiency comes at a much lower cost; however, I want you to remember just how long it can take to develop a new skill because I don't want you to give up on the final stretch of a goal that could change your life. I want you to recognize that the end will always come; it just won't always come as soon as you'd like it to. With that in mind, you need to make sure that you learn how to enjoy the process. Learn to like improving yourself, because you're going to be doing it for your whole life. That said, there's an interesting thing that happens along the way. At some point, you'll start to see the skill in yourself. You won't have achieved mastery yet—you won't have reached your goal quite yet—but you'll have Confidence about what you're doing. You may not even be able to look back and identify a specific moment when you suddenly gained understanding, but you'll know that you know. You'll also still recognize where you need to improve, but that's the point of Momentum. Once you know exactly what you need to work on, you can focus and target your efforts to make them maximally effective.

In fact, that's one of the better descriptions of reaching the point of Momentum. Let me give you an example. My brother has a Ph.D in Biology. To get that degree required years and years of schooling, research, and effort. A couple years ago, I asked my brother to identify the point at which he felt like he knew what he was doing. He replied that he felt Confident once he had the degree—once he'd achieved the goal. I interrupted him and told him to think about it a little more deeply. I asked if he'd felt Confident going into his dissertation. He agreed that he had. I asked him if he'd felt Confident about his research *before* going into his dissertation. He started to see where I was going with my questions and agreed again. As he really thought about it, he couldn't necessarily pin down a specific point at which he became Confident on the journey toward his goal. The answer is that he started to feel Confident once he'd achieved Momentum. He wasn't fully Confident yet—that came after he completed the goal of getting his doctorate—but his Experiences had built him up enough that he'd achieved a level of Confidence. That's the truth of Momentum. It's the growth of Confidence out of Experience, the conversion of *Belief* that you can do something into *Knowledge* that you can do it.

You don't have to put in all 10,000 hours to feel good about yourself or know that you can accomplish a task. Nothing magical happens between the 9,999th and 10,000th hour. You don't put in all those years of effort and then suddenly throw a switch into understanding and Confidence. By trial and error, you'll gain Experience which will gradually progress you through the Belief Blueprint until you reach your goal. When your positive Experiences outweigh your Doubt, you'll tip the scales in the direction of Confidence and begin moving down the slope toward full Confidence and completion of your goal—as long as you don't get distracted by or satisfied with your fledgling Confidence and quit while you're ahead.

Summary

Believe it or not, it's a common problem. People will feel inspired to do something and then, just as that thing starts coming together, they'll move on to the next itch. Don't be so casual about your efforts to achieve self-actualization. There are plenty of things out there you could be doing, but your Why will drive you to the most important ones. Once you figure out your course, stick with the struggle until you reach that point of Momentum where things start to come more easily. Most importantly, don't quit while you're ahead. Don't quit at all. Succeed instead and carry that Momentum into your next goal.

To reach that Momentum point, you need to focus on developing the right kinds of Experience with which to replace your Doubts. You'll reach Momentum once the weight of your positive Experience is more than the weight of your Doubts. That's when you'll start to feel Confidence growing inside, and that Confidence will help you feel like all your effort is paying off—strengthening your resolve. Just don't let the length of the journey dissuade you. Anything worth doing is worth taking time on, so be willing to make that investment and don't cut yourself short.

CONFIDENCE

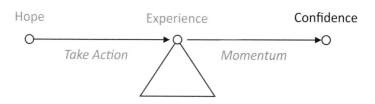

Confidence - [kon-fi-duh ns]
- n. - full trust; belief in the powers, trustworthiness, or reliability of a person or thing[9]

What is Confidence? As you can see from the definition above, Confidence is full trust in something. Confidence is beyond the scope of Hope and into the realm of Knowledge. You are Confident in something when you Know it's going to happen. Once you reach that stage, you no longer need your Hope in that thing because you have a sure Knowledge of it. Your Doubts are gone, and you have no remaining questions in your mind about whether you can or can't do something.

Who Cares?

But why does Confidence matter? As we just talked about in the last chapter, you'll start to build Confidence before you ever reach this final stage, so why spend the extra effort to get this far? What is so special about sticking it out to the finish in order to gain full Confidence? When

---

[9] confidence. Dictionary.com.*Dictionary.com Unabridged.* Random House, Inc. http://dictionary.reference.com/browse/confidence (accessed: February 23, 2015).

we started this journey together, I told you that my hope was to help you become the very best person you could be. What kind of a friend would I be if I let you think you could quit right at the finish line?

Confidence matters because it's the final stage when you can say that you really get it. It's the point at which you can look back and smile at your accomplishment. Confidence is what brings success—not false confidence or bravado but true, deep, honest Confidence born from Experience in the fiery crucible of life. Confidence matters because it's what will confirm you are on the right path to reach your outer limits and then allow you to go beyond them to new heights and distances that you have never dreamed of before. Confidence is what gets things done. And let's be honest here; you picked up this book because you wanted to learn how to become more Confident than you were before. Everything we've been talking about is designed to take you to new levels. Confidence is the ultimate, universal reward for all your work, and it comes as a bonus to whatever other rewards your individual goals bring you.

When I was creating The Belief Blueprint, I spent a lot of time thinking about what to call this level. I considered words like mastery, competence, self-knowledge, and even belief. Ultimately, I decided that Confidence was a more descriptive word for what I had in mind. Mastery implied that you didn't need to learn any more about a topic, but I don't really believe that's ever true. You can have full Confidence in something but still have room to grow. For example, you can be capable of playing any piece on the piano but still not have mastered music. Still, if you have the ability to play anything that someone can put in front of you, you'll be pretty Confident in your ability. You'll be certain of what you can do.

Mastery felt like it went too far. It was promising too much. Competence, on the other hand, felt like it didn't promise enough. It felt weak, like a half-measure. Competence means that you can get the job done, but it implies that you get the job done without any finesse—possibly without even doing it properly. It's kind of like the caveman version of doing something. It's being able to mash the gas pedal or brake and turn the steering wheel without really understanding the finer points of traffic flow or courtesy. Competence is being able to react to the present and stay on top of things. Confidence goes deeper than that, though. Confidence comes when you can see into the possibilities of the future and feel prepared for what it might bring. Competence is really just a waystation along the road to Confidence. Competence is usually reached even before you start to build Momentum.

Self-knowledge didn't work because it was too vague and too inclusive. I can have a perfect knowledge of my inability to say no to sweets without it making me a better person. On the one hand, having that knowledge will help me to know that I need to avoid situations where sweets are served, but how does that really increase or display my Confidence? Basically, I'll be expressing Confidence in my ability to eat sweets—or Confidence that I have no self-control. Neither of those things is really what I had in mind for Confidence. Confidence should be a benefit to you. It should be improvement and growth. Self-knowledge includes Confidence, but it isn't focused enough.

I went through other ideas too, like Belief, but the subject of Belief is more global. Increased confidence in multiple subjects builds your overall Belief. Belief is not Knowledge. But having Confidence in many relevant areas can give you a powerful Belief in something you don't yet have Knowledge in. The term "Confidence" is more specific for what I'm describing in the Belief Blueprint. It also needed to be less technical than terms like self-actualization (which just means growing to a higher plane; making yourself better), so I settled on Confidence because it seemed to include all the parts without getting off topic.

What is Confidence?

So what, exactly, is Confidence? What does it include? According to the simple design of the Belief Blueprint, Confidence is the eventual destination of all your Experience. Every good thing you accomplish or bad thing you struggle through on a certain subject will add up to become your Confidence in that thing. It will be built up by your successes and positive Experiences, cut away and shaped by the bad ones. Ultimately, your Confidence will only be as full as you have positive Experience to make it from. Confidence is the result of consistent, correct effort over time. Confidence is the result of training your limbic brain.

When we talked about achieving goals toward the beginning of the book, we talked about how you need to rally your emotions to support you or you'll never have the tenacity to accomplish anything grand. We talked about how you have three general levels to your brain, and the real power to accomplish things comes from that primal, deep portion of your brain. Your limbic brain is what truly motivates you to do more and become something better, always reaching to fulfill the next pressing need in your life. We also discussed how you can't go in and "change" your limbic brain. It's outside of your conscious control, so you have to approach it differently; you have to approach it through the channels of emotion and attitude. In fact, this whole book is about how to do just that. We've been talking about how to train your limbic brain to work for you. How to train the lion.

Confidence is spending enough time on something that you, in effect, train your "muscle memory" on that thing. You know it so well that your responses become instinctive. It's not just Believing that you can do something, but Knowing that you can do it again and again. This can apply to subjects as simple as learning how to jump rope or as complex as understanding how to design skyscrapers. Once you develop real Confidence, you'll have refined your "knee-jerk" response in any related situation. You'll have trained your gut to "feel" what's right because you'll have had so much Experience that you'll already instinctively know what the outcome will be. That's Confidence.

Fearless

Confidence is fearless too. Why? Because fear stems from Doubt—the unknown, and Confidence has no Doubt left—all relevant aspects are known. When you build enough Experience to hit Momentum and soon thereafter reach Confidence, you'll have replaced all those Doubts with positive Experiences. You'll have answered all the questions and concerns you might have otherwise had. Let me put this into perspective for you.

Let's say you just started a new job for a bank. You're not working on the retail side, though; you're working at the corporate office. You've been to school and gotten a general education in business and finance, but this is your first job with a financial institution. You've been on the job for a week or so when your boss comes to you and asks you to create a report for her. She gives you the details of what she needs and then leaves the task in your hands. Now, you've done some reports and analyses back in school, but nothing with real-world implications. Your boss is going to use your report to help her make important decisions. If you screw up, you could do real damage to your team, your department, and your company—not to mention your reputation and possibly your future in the industry. That's a lot of weight to bear.

Because it's your first time doing this kind of report outside the placebo Experience of school, you get started right away and put all your effort into it. Once you think you have it ready, you go to your boss for feedback and instruction. She looks through and mentors you on some of the things you misunderstood. You go back and fix them and turn in the report. Fast-forward a few weeks or a month and your boss comes to you for that report again.

This time, you remember all the things you learned last time around. Building on those prior Experiences, you try again. Then, like before, you go to your boss to make sure you're on the right page. She looks it over and gives you a few areas to reconsider. You go back and clean the report up before turning it in. After a few iterations of this, you'll get to the point where you no longer feel the need to go and have your boss review the report first. Interestingly, you'll probably reach that point just after your boss reaches the point that she no longer feels the need to error-check your work. Once she doesn't really find anything wrong with your report anymore, she will encourage you to just take care of it on your own. By that time, your own fears and insecurities about creating the report will also be fading.

You'll have been through the process enough times—you'll have Taken Action to gain Experience enough times—that you'll have answered your own questions. You'll have resolved your concerns and washed away your Doubts, erasing your fears. With that critical mass of Experience pushing you along, you'll have gained Confidence. The Belief Blueprint has worked yet again to bring you Confidence in this one thing, thereby building your Belief in related future opportunities and goals. What if your boss asked you to create another report using a completely different data set? Would you have full Confidence in being able to do it correctly? Not likely. But your aggregate Belief will be high enough to spark massive Hope, launching the Belief Blueprint forward, drawing on all past Experience and earned Confidence, ultimately landing you in full Confidence shortly thereafter.

Understanding

The key here is that Confidence has understanding. Fear stems from the spaces between your knowledge and Experience. Fear comes from knowing that you don't know what will happen—from uncertainty. When you have fear, it's because you don't have a reasonable expectation of the outcome. Anything could happen, and plenty of the options are bad for you. That's what creates Doubt in the first place. Doubt is the unresolved question in your head of whether it's better to just walk away rather than take the risk or not. What's interesting about Doubt is that those conversations don't really take place in reality, only in between our right and left ears. If you were to actually put those conversations in words and recite them out loud to friends or family (or even perfect strangers), you'd probably feel silly. In fact, you should try it sometime just to see.

Fear is the limbic brain's emotional response to unresolved, negative questions and possible answers in your neocortex. "Just live to see another day," it seems to say. "This just isn't worth the risk!" As you gain understanding, those questions will be answered correctly and go away. The accumulation of understanding—gained through Experience—is what gives rise to your Confidence. Confidence is understanding something well enough that you know you can deal with anything that might come up. You don't necessarily think it will be *easy* to deal with the things that come up, but you know that you'll be able to work your way through in time.

In that way, Confidence also involves knowing your own limitations and how to work around them while simultaneously helping you focus elsewhere. Thinking about your limitations and shortcomings all the time is not a good way to develop Confidence. In fact, it will do just the opposite. Instead, Confidence is accepting your faults and looking for ways to make them irrelevant.

As you already know, I was a nervous kid—and occasionally that showed up even in my teens and into my twenties. Fear of the unknown resulted in sometimes debilitating anxiety. I loved the thrill of presenting and performing, but my nerves inhibited me once in a while. Over time, I was able to work through that. Today, I can get up and speak, comfortably, in front of tens of thousands of people. How did that change come about? I developed Confidence through understanding. I spent time learning and educating myself regarding the topics I was going to cover—to make sure I have the data I need to answer questions and resolve the concerns of others. I also started small and worked my way up. I first started with things like choirs and bands where I could be on the stage performing, but I wasn't alone. I added to that the Experience of talking to small groups. I started with just a couple people at a time, and then went to a handful, then a dozen, then 50, and so on. I didn't start with an audience of 10,000; I built my way up to that point. This gave me the chance to face my fears and resolve them on a smaller scale before taking the next baby step up.

Fruitful

Confidence will grow up just like that. You gain Confidence in one little thing and then leverage it into ever-greater things until you reach your true goal. That's the process of building Momentum that we talked about in the last chapter. Confidence doesn't just grow up for no reason though. Remember that Momentum is mass times velocity. Confidence is the outcome of Momentum, and it carries that same weight and speed forward. For that reason, Confidence doesn't like to stand still. Confidence doesn't want to sit and do nothing.

Confidence wants to be doing things. It wants to be leveraged to stretch and grow. Have you ever noticed how, once you realize you can do something, you want to go out and do it again? There's a novelty and excitement to doing things that you thought were beyond your ability—especially when you thought those things were far beyond your ability. Each time you repeat the same task, that novelty wears away and your Confidence starts to look for something new. It starts to look for the next challenge to rise up against. This pattern of tackling new challenges and overcoming them is a hallmark of Confidence. I call it the fruits of Confidence.

Let me put it to you this way. When you're presented with something that terrifies you, do you want to get involved? If someone suggests that you change the oil in your car but you've never done it before, you might shrink in fear and point out that you have a mechanic for such things. If, however, you learned how to change oil from a parent, friend, sibling, or other relative, you won't bat an eye. You have the Confidence to know that you can change the oil because you've done it before. You might not have the time to do it right then, but you certainly aren't afraid of going out and doing it. In fact, part of you will even want to go out and change the oil just to remind yourself that you can do it—to prove it to yourself again. Confidence will drive you to action that way. Confidence doesn't shy away.

This is why, when you look around at all the people you know, the ones who seem most Confident also seem to be the ones who are making progress and getting things done. These people know they can accomplish what they want, so they go out and do it. They don't sit there trying to weigh the pros and cons. They aren't concerned with the politics and deliberations that some people frame around every decision. They also aren't the ones who talk big and play small. These aren't the high-pressure salespeople who are desperate to push another sale. This is the person who's willing to take time to answer your questions and resolve your concerns, knowing that you'll buy when you're ready. Because he or she has plenty of clients like you, there's no rush to push someone into a close today. Confidence doesn't need to be loud because the results will speak for themselves.

What Confidence Isn't

Which brings up another important point. Confidence has gotten a bit of a strange name recently. Like so many things in society today, we've twisted the word around and around until no one is really sure what it's supposed to mean. We understand that Confidence is a good thing, but even that truth is under attack in some ways. For example, when we think of "confident" people, we often think of the loud, in-your-face types. We think of people who seem to be fearless and willing to do anything. I'm not saying that those people aren't confident, but I am saying that those characteristics are not indicative of Confidence, not on their own anyway. Yet society would have us believe that these obnoxious people are a random sample of Confident people, making Confidence somewhat less desirable. Society is wrong.

Confidence doesn't need to be loud because Confidence doesn't need the recognition of others. People with real Confidence are secure in themselves. They don't need external praise or validation. They like to be thanked and like to be praised as much as the next person, but they don't *need* it. They aren't doing what they do in order to earn the accolades (unless their Why is external praise, which is the case for some people). People with real Confidence do what they need to do in order to secure their respective Whys regardless of what everyone else is doing or saying. So let's take a look at a few of the things society tries to equate with Confidence and why those things are nothing but flimsy counterfeits. I do this in order to help you differentiate within yourself between real Confidence and counterfeit Confidence.

Blind Follower

It's a very good thing to have people that you trust enough to know that you can do what they ask without question and without danger to yourself. Ideally your family and friends fit this mold. Either way, there's a certain movement in society to "look the part" of Confidence by simply doing what everyone else does. People are trying to stand out from each other, yet they're all doing the same things to stand out. You could compare these people to a herd of zebra. It's easy to spot zebra in the wild, but in the herd situation it's difficult to tell where one ends and the next begins.

In modern society, you can look at the "thought leaders" and "culture leaders" who have some level of Confidence. In an effort to be more like those icons, normal people like you and me will sometimes pick up different mannerisms or outward shows. Someone might dress the same way as a famous actor or actress, for instance. Someone might read all the same books as a famous CEO (or at least pretend to read the same books). The sad thing is, in trying to replicate someone else's Confidence, these people are betraying their own Confidence. They are undermining themselves by telling themselves that someone else's way of doing things is more valid than their own. This is basically a self-imposed disconnect from that individual's Why in favor of pursuing the appearance of someone else's Why. That doesn't do much to boost Confidence; it breeds Doubt and Despair instead. Is it any wonder that the medical condition of depression is on the rise? Remember that inspiration without expression is depression. Expression of borrowed or false inspiration is the equivalent of not expressing it at all. It does no good in moving you toward your own inspiration—your Core Why.

Shortcutting

One of the biggest pitfalls is that people don't want to go through the whole Belief Blueprint as I've explained it to you. They want the reward of Confidence without all the effort and energy involved in gaining the Experience. For many, the desire for Confidence is so strong that they'll just pretend instead. Some of them pretend with the intention of gaining the requisite Experience along the way. Others dispense with that and just embrace the lie, acting like they can shortcut their way to Confidence. You probably know someone like this. He acts like he knows what he's doing but then he never quite seems to come through on anything. Instead, he's always got an excuse for why he couldn't follow through and why he needs someone else to pick up the slack.

The truth is that he doesn't know what he's doing but he doesn't want anyone else to know it. This desire to hide the truth can make these people dangerous. They will do whatever they can to not come clean. And the longer they keep up the ruse the more dangerous they become because people around them will actually start to believe that there's some truth to the lie—at least until evidence surfaces to the contrary.

In this era of cut-and-paste viral online sharing, there are far too many examples where the statements of inexperienced but opinionated individuals are passed along without fact-checking or verifying credentials of the writer, and it's not until days or weeks later that the information is exposed as false or at the very least misguided. Even top government officials have been fooled into sharing the ramblings of falsely confident bloggers or editorial writers who lack the real Experience to add validity to their writing.

The truth is there are no shortcuts to building real Confidence. You have to start with step one and move to step two. You can't skip anything along the way or you'll leave gaps and vulnerabilities in your Confidence. Instead of building yourself up to be strong and independent, you'll be building yourself into a pretty storefront with nothing valuable inside. This is like putting beautiful frosting on a cake made of Styrofoam. Everything looks good until you get under the surface and see the reality.

Overconfident

Next on the list is everyone's favorite. Similar to the people who are trying to shortcut the process, some people simply take more credit than they deserve. In their defense, at least they're actually doing something. These people are going through the process; they just believe they're further along than they really are. One of the big differences between these people and the shortcutters is that the overconfident ones actually believe they're as good as they say they are. Shortcutters know that they're lying. Overconfident people don't know that they're living a fantasy.

This break from the reality of the situation makes them simultaneously more and less dangerous than the shortcutters. Overconfident people have convinced themselves that they deserve all the confidence for very little work, usually citing their own raw talent as a source of success. As a result, they won't try to cover for themselves (at least initially) because they don't think there will be a problem. They honestly believe that they're up to the task, so they don't see the need to hedge their bets. This makes them less dangerous because they're more likely to screw up earlier on and reveal the truth about themselves. For some people, that first big screw-up is enough to wake them up to the reality of the situation, humble them, and get them back on track.

At the same time, these people can be more dangerous because they don't know what they don't know. Their overconfidence can often drive them to do things they aren't ready for—often with disastrous consequences. Shortcutters at least realize that they've skipped a step, and they'll find ways to avoid putting that shortcoming on display. They'll try to avoid doing things that they know they can't do, which means they're less likely to take up an important position and then fail. They'd much rather fake things from the sidelines than get in the game and get crushed for fumbling a play.

False Hope

This next one is a little strange yet somewhat similar to the blind followers we talked about a moment ago. Rather than dealing directly with Confidence, this one is about how some people choose to give themselves over to false Hope. False Hope isn't the same as hoping for something unlikely—like a small bill at the mechanic's when your car breaks down. False Hope is when you Hope for something you already Know isn't true. This is more like hoping that your car will magically be untouched after you crash it into a telephone pole.

The problem with false Hope is that you can't build real Experience and Confidence on it. Your confirmation bias will do all kinds of wonderful things to help you think that your Hope is valid, but you'll already know it isn't. In order to build on that Hope, you'll have to ignore yourself and the reality around you. That willful ignorance will prevent you from really gaining valid Experience because you'll be pursuing something that doesn't really exist. Your Experience will just end up helping you get better at fooling yourself. Eventually, you'll be living in a reality so different from that of everyone else that you won't be able to function properly. Your false Hope will turn your life sideways and take you places that don't really exist.

All the hoping in the world won't make it true. So don't waste your time trying to Hope for things you already know are false. That's a quick way to break from reality and lose your ability to make any real progress or real self-improvement. Instead, find ways to leverage your real Hope to make your future happen. By harnessing your Why—a

Why that lines up with reality—you can build Experience and Confidence and shape your future to be what you want it to be.

Arrogance

Last but not least, I need to define something that most people don't clearly understand. For some reason, arrogance and Confidence are now synonymous in today's society. I'm not sure how or when that happened, but it did, and I don't like it one bit! If you know what you're doing because you have actual Experience in it (not because you say you know), you have Confidence. Unfortunately, people who *don't* know what you're doing might be jealous of your ability. For that reason, they will say things about how you're showing off or how you're being arrogant or cocky. Their words have no bearing on the reality of your Confidence and Experience, but they will say things anyway to soothe their own battered pride. The truth is, they don't understand what arrogance and Confidence really are.

Confidence is quiet. It's self-monitoring and self-moderating. Confidence grows from Experience and entails the ability to act and react in a given situation because you already Know what the outcome will be and what your ability level is. Confidence exists in a vacuum. It doesn't push to the outside and it can't be pushed from the outside. It just *is*. And that's where society goes wrong when it tries to blur the lines defining confidence.

Arrogance, on the other hand, is loud, obnoxious, conceited, condescending, and self-important. Arrogance is Confidence gone bad. In order to be truly arrogant, not just overconfident, you have to have Experience that supports your attitude. You have to have gone through the same kinds of things that would bring you Confidence. The difference is that arrogance can't exist on its own. Arrogance requires a constant influx of outside input. Where Confidence is gained and retained forever, arrogance must be maintained forever. In the simplest terms, arrogance is lording Confidence over someone else. It's twisting your Confidence into a weapon, rather than a tool. Arrogance is like unfulfilled, unrealized Confidence. You've gained all the Experience, but you can't feel Confident in that Experience unless you can rub it in the face of someone who hasn't been through the same thing.

In effect, arrogance still has something to prove where Confidence has already proven it. That's why arrogance is so frustrating to see. You look at an arrogant person and know that the person has a wealth of Experience, but you also know that he or she is completely unwilling to share any kind of learning with anyone else. They refuse to mentor or truly lead or do anything other than hoard up more Experience and knowledge for themselves. It's like the lessons of Experience are somehow perishable or limited in distribution. It's a scarcity mindset. Arrogant people also refuse to share their knowledge with anyone else because they perceive that their knowledge gives them power over others. Sadly, this sets them up to actually erode their own Confidence right out from underneath themselves. They've Taken Action and earned the Experience, but then they corrupted that Experience by twisting it into something worthless, robbing themselves of true Confidence. Arrogance is truly a sad state of being.

Your Confidence Will Carry You

The beauty of Confidence is that it's the wholesome completion of Experience, and like Experience, Confidence is yours forever. Any given Experience can help to move you forward through the Belief Blueprints you're working on for any number of different goals and objectives, but previously earned Confidence gives you a far bigger step. Not only that, Confidence in one thing will inevitably spill over and help you build velocity in everything else. The more things in your life you're Confident about, the more quickly you'll work to gain additional Confidence because you'll be more accustomed to pushing through your Doubts and Taking Action to gain Experience. For example, if you've gained Confidence in sports during high school or college, you can carry that over into your work life. Confidence gained through dating can help you find an employer, and vice versa. The reason is simply that knowing you're good at something strengthens your inner core, making you less susceptible to the hurricanes and whirlwinds of life.

In effect, each new thing you gain Confidence in will help you to root yourself. The more you know you can do, the more stable you'll be when you try new things. You'll also be more stable when critics or setbacks come at you. If you don't have any of that Confidence, you won't be grounded and affirmed by your Experience and victories, and you will be that much more likely to get pushed around by life. Having Confidence can get you through anything life throws at you. I'm not saying that life's challenges will be easy just because of the Confidence you've gained, but they will certainly be eas*ier*. The process of gaining Confidence will leave you accustomed to Taking Action and investing time and effort. You'll also have that inner Belief in yourself and your ability to overcome. Those things will work together to help you overcome what life puts in your path.

Over time, each bit of Confidence you gain will be like another drop in your bucket, adding weight to your personality. Given enough time and focus on your part, you can actually build up a vast ocean of Confidence and positive Experience, growing aggregate Belief. With that pushing behind you, you'll become unstoppable in accomplishing the things your Why drives you toward. Just remember that it doesn't happen overnight. It takes years and years and even decades of focus and effort and patience, but it will come if you keep Taking Action and working at it. You just have to stay strong and focused on your Why. It will give you the strength to continue forward and build that Confidence.

Exploding at the Finish

For example, sometimes you'll start on a new venture, make it really far into the process and then realize that you're doing the wrong thing. I call this exploding at the finish, and it's a very interesting situation to look at. I've told you time and again to not quit right at the end, and I mean it. Too many people pursue their Why for nine tenths of the way—only to quit in sight of the finish line. Now, in their defense, they probably couldn't see the finish line. Still, they make it almost the whole way there before giving in to despair and quitting. They give up on their Why and walk away. Don't ever do that. Don't give up on your

Why. It's your core driver. You need to harness your Why if you want to become your best self.

Exploding at the finish is a quick way to waste all that time and effort. Sure the Experience you gained will stick with you and help you with your other goals on a low level, but quitting at the end will color all that Experience and cut into any Confidence you might have gained along the way. This would be like training for a marathon only to sit down after mile 26 on race day. Just two tenths of a mile from the finish after all that hard work, and you'd be left with basically nothing to show for it. Worse yet, giving up on that magnitude can leave your limbic brain weak, or at least your connection to it. You'll lose some of the capacity for connecting with your Why. In a way, you'll actually gain *negative* Confidence. You'll reinforce a knowledge within yourself that you're actually a failure.

This is clearly a bad thing. It's the exact opposite of the progress we're trying to make in this book. If you get in a bind and have to put the brakes on a goal, you'd better immediately sit down and commit to an action plan to get yourself back on track and going again—including specifics on just how long your break is going to be. Don't risk giving up your Momentum in its entirety. You fought so hard to gain it in the first place; if you blow your Momentum at the end, it can be harder than ever to get going again, leading to you exploding at the finish. So, if you have to pause for any reason, set your action plan and commit to it. Just like starting out on a brand new goal, be sure to tell everyone about your plans and turn them all into your personal accountability partners. Anything you can do to increase your motivation for getting back on track when the time comes will help you to save up a portion of that Momentum so you don't have to start over from scratch.

The best course of action is to simply not stop once you start, but I understand that life happens, situations change, and people have to put things on hold from time to time—even important things. Just remember that you can only be moving forward or backward. No one can ever take your Experience from you, but time can dull the weight of it (thankfully it dulls the negative Experience at a faster rate). So again, build up your Momentum and ride it through to Confidence. Don't stop the train somewhere out on the tracks if you can help it.

Switching Tracks

Still, in some cases there is a reason to change directions. Notice that I didn't say give up. You should never give up on a goal if it's aligned with your Why. If you make a goal that doesn't align with who you are (out of peer pressure or in a careless moment or for some other reason), you can re-evaluate those goals. However, if something is aligned with your Why (like it should be), you literally can't give up on it. That said, sometimes you'll get on down the path before you realize that the vehicle you've chosen no longer serves you. Sometimes you can even put in significant amounts of time and effort before you realize that your Why is pulling you in a new direction. You shouldn't spend your time mourning the pending course change, but embracing the squiggle we all experience on the journey from point A to point B.

Let me give you an example of this. My sister loved ballet when she was growing up. She loved the expression in the movements, and she didn't just love to watch it. She took ballet lessons. She loved to dance and she loved to perform. For a lot of years she took ballet lessons, but things started to change, and over time it became a less ideal art form for her. She loved ballet. She was good at ballet. She'd developed a lot of Confidence in her ability to dance ballet, but adolescence changed her physical form enough that continuing would prove more challenging than before, and she and many other girls in the dance company began receiving extremely restrictive dietary guidelines from a new instructor. At that point in her progression, the next step into the ballet company would also demand much more time, eliminating her ability to pursue any other interests. On top of that, my parents came to her with the news that she needed to choose just one set of lessons as finances were limited at the time. Now, she could have fought through it and found a way to make it work, like when my wife fought against Achilles tendinitis, but my sister made a different valid choice. She wasn't interested in forcing herself to become the kind of body type preferred in higher levels of ballet. She had other interests that aligned more closely with what she really wanted in life and she decided to change her focus to taking voice lessons. So, with memorable resolve, she packed up her Confidence, and began to apply her energy and ability to developing her beautiful singing voice.

Some people would call this giving up right at the end, but the truth is that she had never intended to be a ballerina as a profession. She loved ballet, but it was a wonderful hobby, and it was time to move on. More importantly, she didn't leave her Confidence behind. She didn't hang her head in defeat and give up on her dreams. She'd been living her dreams for years, and she was ready to go and live a new dream. It's important to note that she has had far more opportunities to sing and share her voice talent, something she loves to do, more than she ever could have with ballet.

The point of this example is that sometimes this happens. Sometimes we board a train bound for a distant destination only to realize that this train won't take us all the way. There are really just a couple options when this happens. You can get off and go home, or you can change trains.

Obviously, turning around and going home is quitting. It's failure. Don't go there. You started off on this journey because it aligned with your Why, right? So figure out how you can get back to alignment and keep going. Don't just sit down by the tracks and give up.

The alternative is to switch trains. You know you started in the correct general direction, so why give that up? Then again, you've also learned that you're not going quite the right way. The solution then is to alter course. You can keep moving but shift your target. You don't need to depart from your Why by accident or by design. Goals often evolve over time. Remember the path to success is never a straight line. I told you about my goal to get a Dodge Viper. My goal isn't really about the car anymore because I've learned that the car isn't really my Why. My Why is financial security, and the car is just a representation of that. At some point, I looked at that car on my vision board and realized that it wasn't my Why. I didn't give up and I didn't go out and buy it anyway; I figured out where my Why was really taking me and kept moving. My sister did the same thing when she dropped ballet and refocused her efforts elsewhere.

She didn't give up on her Why either. In fact, she probably stayed truer to it by leaving ballet behind than if she'd tried to tough it out. I don't know her Why exactly, but I would guess it wasn't dance. And since dance wasn't her Why anyway, she looked at it and reassessed how she could pursue her Why outside the realm of ballet. As it turns out, ballet had been a great thing for her for a lot of years, but it was no longer the right vehicle for getting her to where she wanted to go. That happens frequently in life, though people don't often know it, and it's a signal that you might be on the wrong train.

The Right Vehicle

The beauty of gaining Confidence is that you'll know when you've reached your connection and it's time to switch trains. People with no Confidence will continue to pursue the same fruitless things forever (usually easy ones, like video games with endless levels of intangible achievements), but people with Confidence use different vehicles to pursue greater Confidence without fear of locking themselves in. I actually had this happen to me with jobs twice in a row after I got out of college.

Fresh out of my business undergraduate program, I landed something of a dream job. I was hired by a family-owned company that had a number of different real-estate investments. They owned water parks, apartment buildings, and other similar properties. Talk about plunging me into the deep end. I went from being a student to commanding hundreds of thousands of dollars of marketing budget. I had to do the research and figure out not only where to advertise and what demographics to target and what mediums to use, but also which properties to boost. It was a steep learning curve, but I was determined. I had plenty of Confidence from prior things I'd done, so I didn't hesitate to jump in and get to work—and I made some good things happen, as well as some rookie mistakes along the way. In the process of riding that train and gaining that Experience and Confidence, I took the chance to mentor others who were newer in the organization. I was hoping that I could help them be more efficient and that, in turn, they'd help me back. It didn't work out that way.

Eventually, I caught on to the fact that I had somehow been blacklisted. I wasn't going to be getting any new promotions or, more importantly, new responsibilities and challenges. Once I made that connection, I naturally became aware that I would need a new vehicle. Had I failed at my job? No. I hadn't performed below the expectations placed on me. I had worked hard and learned a lot, generating a lot of new revenue and good will from those properties. At the same time, my performance had built me up, taught me, and increased my Confidence. I had learned and grown enough that even being faced with direct antagonism from some of my friends and colleagues didn't shut me up or put me down—even if it did hurt.

I can remember one meeting in particular; we were sitting around brainstorming about a new internal management program. It was going to be a leadership think tank type of thing, and we were deciding who would be involved. Then we moved on to the part where we nominated people to become future company leaders. That meeting, believe it or not, devolved into a roast with most of the other people in the room trying to convince me that I wasn't the right personality fit for the group. I remember sitting there for more than an hour while people took turns trying to pick me apart. I also remember talking through each of their arguments and refuting them. Still, by the end things were pretty obvious.

It wasn't but a few days later that I met an extremely talented business woman who spontaneously invited me to take on a key role (and ownership) in her fast-growing start-up company. A start-up meant that there would be tremendous growth potential—both for the new company and for me personally. It was a complete shift in what I thought my career path would be. But after a couple weeks of careful consideration, vetting the new company's financials, structure, and strategy, I signed on, bringing all my Confidence with me. I knew what I was good at, and I knew what I wasn't good at. I also knew how to focus my efforts where I could do the most good, so I did just that. I had learned and developed all of that during school and during that first job. I still didn't feel great about what had just happened prior to leaving the real estate management company, but my real Confidence was unassailable because it was grounded deep in past results—positive Experiences and successes. At this new company, I was able to rub shoulders with powerful people, successful people. I remember sitting in a room with billionaires and listening to them, learning from them.

After an exciting couple of years, a merger, some large cash offers, and some changes in upper management, I realized that the company wasn't growing like we'd hoped. Some of our competitors had gotten some strategic advantages in the industry and were edging us out of much needed funding. I realized that for the foreseeable future my income and personal progression were going to remain fairly stationary. That's when I received another job offer. At first I was hesitant. I wasn't really certain which path would best match my Why. I spent a lot of time thinking about it, meditating and praying about it. Ultimately, my wife and I decided that it was time to move on. The new opportunity had a better chance of giving me the kind of freedom and flexibility that I wanted while still providing for my family. It was a better fit for my Why. Months later I realized that my Why had been bringing me to this point all along, gently guiding me along the path to fulfilling my deepest needs.

The same can happen for you. When it does, take a moment to consider your options. Go back to your Why. Which vehicle is the right one to get you to your destination? Keeping in mind that what was the right vehicle in the past might not be exactly right anymore, or that there could be multiple good options. Once you've figured out which vehicle better aligns with your Why, the decision will be easy to make because your limbic brain will be carrying you forward. You just have to trust that you've trained your gut. You just have to recognize the Confidence you've developed.

Just Add Time

As you move from one vehicle to the next—either because you've taken the train to the end of the line or because you're adjusting your focus and jumping to a new train—you will be creating a long string of victories. Confidence points. You'll be filling up that ocean with all of your drops of success. And that's the best definition of personal development that I can think of. Personal development is the ongoing process of obtaining Confidence in different aspects of life. It's tipping the seesaw in the Belief Blueprint time and time again while working on goal after goal.

Confidence reaffirms your Why and strengthens your resolve to continue on to newer, bigger, harder, more complex goals and aspirations. The more Confidence you gain, the more developed you'll be to take on the next challenge. Personal development, then, is actually seeking out those opportunities to gain Confidence and capitalizing on them when you find them. You can think of it almost like an exercise plan for your Confidence. You create your list of goals and aspirations in line with your Why and then start working on them, building yourself up and becoming the person you want to be. It's not an easy process any more than going to the gym regularly is easy (and if going to the gym *is* easy, you might not be pushing yourself), but it's a worthwhile process because it will add value to your life.

Just remember that you can't cram development any more than you can cram exercise. You have to stick with it over time to get real results. Going to a motivational speaker and then going home and forgetting about it will do nothing for you. Reading this book but never acting on anything you've read will do nothing for you. The key is Action over time. As you do that, you'll develop yourself into the person you've always wanted to be.

Summary

Confidence, in the end, is the power to accomplish great things gained by accomplishing other things. You achieve it by tipping the seesaw in the Belief Blueprint through gaining Experience. Once you have it, it's yours forever and can help you to push forward on everything else in your life, but Confidence doesn't really take credit for that. Confidence isn't about being better than anyone except for the person you were yesterday. It's secure in itself and doesn't need external validation or input. In fact, Confidence just exists and needs nothing else— though it will drive you to accomplish even more. Personal development is that act of setting goals and seeking out growth—of doing more and seeking more Confidence. As you develop yourself, you will gain that quiet, powerful inner core which will keep you strong when the world seems to turn against you. It's the process of aligning with your powerful limbic lion.

True Confidence is immutable, but there are plenty of counterfeits out there to make it harder to identify the right path and gain real

Confidence. Things like arrogance, false Hope, and overconfidence can rob you of true Confidence by making it harder to get the right kind of Experience and harder to see how that Experience applies in your life. If you want to be successful, you need to stay focused. Make sure you know where you're going rather than just following the crowd with blind faith. Also avoid anything that appears to be a shortcut to Confidence. Real Confidence can only be gained through effort over time. There are no shortcuts.

The key is to just get started and move your feet in the right direction. As you go, you'll refine your vision and gain a better understanding of your Why. That self-improvement will generate Confidence within you and help you to better target your efforts to gain ever greater Confidence and more effectively seek your Whys, leading to self-actualization, success, and lasting peace and happiness. You'll be tipping the seesaw in your favor, and it'll stay tipped there. Forever.

PUTTING IT TOGETHER

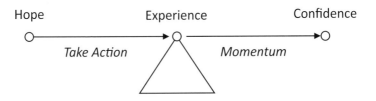

Congratulations! We've now been through all the phases of The Belief Blueprint. Hopefully you have a better understanding of how your mind works and why you Experience things in different ways than the people around you. You know how your Hope can be leveraged into Confidence—your Belief into Knowledge. You now know how to train your limbic brain to make your knee-jerk reactions take you to where you want to go. You have the general information, but there are a few more details I'd like to explain. These are things that pertain to the entire model at the same time, so I thought I should save them until you understood the entire model. To that end, I'm going to start with an example that brings the whole thing together.

Mountain Climbing

Imagine that you're standing at the bottom of a tall, rugged mountain. You can see the trail winding up for some distance before it disappears into the scrubby foliage and rocky outcroppings that decorate the side of the towering mountain in front of you. It's early fall, but at this altitude, the leaves are already starting to lose the green of summer and explode into the vibrant reds, yellows, and oranges of autumn. In some places, it's almost like the side of the mountain is ablaze with plant life. The view is breathtaking. Awe inspiring. Daunting.

Hope

You've never taken this particular hike before, but you've been walking and you've been on other hikes. You haven't done the *exact* same thing in the past, but you've done other similar things, and that helps you to Believe that you can make it. What's more, you have a craving for adventure, and this mountain has been calling to you for years now. You've always considered trying to hike it, but you've just never been able to fit in the time and attention. Now you can, and you're going to prove to yourself that you can do this difficult thing. You Hope that you can tackle the challenge and come out stronger for it, and you're ready to prove that Hope true.

Somewhere, up and over that snow-capped peak is the trail that leads down the far side—the trail that leads to your finish. It's a long, hard hike you've planned for yourself, but the day is perfect for it. The sky is clear and vibrant blue. The breeze is rustling through the trees, stirring the aroma of the soil warming under the sun. You've packed plenty of water and food for the journey, you've got a map and your GPS to keep you on the trail, and you brought a jacket for when it gets cold. Everything's ready to go and the adventure beckons to you.

Take Action

Now is when you face that first, difficult step. You're standing at the edge of the parking lot, and it's not too late to turn back. Your ride is still waiting behind you—your connection back to the relative safety and security of the status quo. You have a choice of stepping out onto the hard-packed dirt of the trail or of turning back. Climbing up and over this mountain isn't going to mean anything to anyone else. This is your thing, and no one else is going to understand what you've done or why it is important to you. Not the way you will, anyway. You know the way ahead won't be easy—it may even be dangerous at points—but your Hope tells you that the views and experiences you'll have will all be worth it. What are you going to do?

In line with your commitment to yourself, you take that first step. Your boot crunches softly on the loose dirt of the path, and you're off. That wasn't so hard, right? You had a moment of hesitation and indecision, but it passed. Now you're on your way. Ahead of you, you'll face untold wonders and challenges, but you're Taking Action and moving forward. Each step brings a new experience to you. You can feel the muscles of your legs working to move you forward and upward. Your back and shoulders are working to support the load of your supplies. Your heart is pounding and your lungs are burning with the effort of supplying your body with the thinner mountain air you need to keep pushing forward. Your blood is racing, and you feel alive in spite of the difficulty of the winding, rough path.

Initially, you have all the energy of your Belief to fuel you, but that starts to burn away after an hour or so. Pretty soon, you can feel doubts starting to creep into your mind. You might even look back and try to find the parking lot, but your ride is long gone by now. You need to push forward on your own, and you haven't seen what you came to see yet. It doesn't help that the trail seems to wind back and forth across the face of the mountain, going from side to side without seeming to go up much. It feels like you'd be able to make better time if you just went straight up the side instead.

Then you come back around another switchback and realize that you're skirting the top of a sheer cliff you hadn't noticed before. You're safe on top and you'd be safe below, but trying to come straight up the mountain would have put you right into the cliff face. You only avoided it because you allowed yourself to follow the mountain. And then you look out over the valley below and realize how high you've come. Still, you can see the parking lot full of tiny toy cars below you but you can't see the peak way up overhead. It's lost from view, and that means it's farther than the parking lot. It's tempting to turn back, but you don't want to give up now, even if you can feel the effects of the altitude and the strain of the hike wearing into your stamina. You're pretty sure you can make it, but you're starting to wonder if it's worth it.

Just then you come around another corner and freeze in your tracks. Tucked into the side of the mountain is an old avalanche chute, an alpine meadow stretching up a fold in the rock. Wildflowers fill the meadow and, even in the cool of the autumn morning, you can hear the humming of bees in the air as they hurry to finish their work before the chill of winter sets in. The sight of all those colors painting the side of the mountain nearly takes your breath away. You can't help but wonder what other secret treasures the mountain might hold for you before you reach the end of your hike. You certainly never expected everything you've seen so far.

Experience

You reach the snowcapped peak right at lunchtime. It's been a brutal hike, but the things you've Experienced could never be replaced. You look forward to telling your family and friends about some of the things you've seen, and even though the hike has been hard and your legs are tired, you're glad you came. From where you are, you can see the mountain spreading out below you in all directions. You can see the tangle of mountains and valleys around you with their avalanche chutes and alpine forests. You can see the path you took scrawling out below you—most of it anyway. You can also see a couple other paths that you didn't know existed before. Apparently other people have taken the same hike but by different methods.

Your Experience in climbing up the mountain has also given you a better perspective on what it's going to take to get down the other side. You know things won't be exactly the same on the second half of the journey, but they should be fairly similar. From what you can see of the path going down the other side, it shouldn't be any more difficult than what you've already faced. And at least you'll be able to better see where you're going now. The path will be more obvious down below you as you move forward instead of being hidden somewhere above you. All in all, your Hope is stronger than ever that you'll be able to make it.

The wind is cutting up over the peak with a bitter chill, so you pause to put on your jacket. Then you decide to have your lunch in the shelter of a large boulder before starting on the second half of your hike. While you're eating, you think about the rock slides you've had to scramble over, the streams you've had to cross, the stunning vistas you've seen, and the animals you've witnessed sharing the mountainside. There were plenty of times when you wondered if it was all too hard—even a few close calls—but you managed to hold out for the next breathtaking view each time. When you'd started out, you Hoped you had the endurance to make it to the end of the hike, and now you know you had the stamina to at least reach the peak. The good news is, it's all downhill from here, right? After your lunch, you decide you'd better get moving again before you freeze.

Momentum

Starting out again, it's all you can do to stop yourself from sliding down the snowy path. You thought coming down the mountain would be easier, but it turns out to be only faster. You almost have to be even more careful about where you put your feet and how you pace yourself. Still, all that time climbing up the backside of the mountain has prepared you for this. You know where to place your feet when the trail looks loose and dangerous. You know how to step from rock to rock in order to avoid putting your feet in the streams you cross. You've been doing all this already, so now it's just a matter of doing what you already know, and you have gravity on your side now.

You do catch yourself wanting to run forward a few times—especially down the longer straightaways, but after one harrowing Experience you decide not to try that again. You didn't realize how easy it would be to nearly lose control on the way down, and the switchbacks don't have banked curves to help you keep in control. That's up to you. So you focus on keeping your feet under control and keeping them going in the right direction. The switchbacks make a lot more sense to you now too. If you were to try to shortcut straight down the side of the mountain, there's no way you'd be able to stay in control. You'd probably end up triggering a rock slide and ending your hike prematurely—and maybe permanently!

What surprises you is just how much effort it takes to keep going. You'd expected the downhill side to be easy, but it's not. Your muscles still have to work just as hard to take each step, but your Hope is burning bright again, fueling you. You already made it up and over the peak. There's nothing else the mountain can throw at you to stop you or make you turn back. In fact, the idea of turning back is probably enough to make you feel a little sick, so you just push on and put one foot in front of the other.

Confidence

Finally, just as the sun is painting the sky with reds and golds in the west, you reach the ending parking lot. You almost collapse in relief at reaching your destination. It took a lot out of you, but you made it anyway. Your car is there waiting for you. You trudge across the asphalt and stop at the driver's door to get your keys out. Just then, you have a thought. Your mind is filled with a slideshow of the amazing things you witnessed on the slopes. You look forward to telling others all about your adventure, but you know they'll never fully understand until they come and try it for themselves. Still, you've learned things about yourself. You've tested your limits and stretched them. You've made yourself stronger than you were before, and the mountain behind you is proof of your accomplishment.

You turn back and look up at the mountain, admiring its sunset glow. Looking back, you can hardly believe that you actually made it over such a huge obstacle, but your tired and achy feet reassure you that the journey was real. The process of conquering that mountain wore you down to almost nothing at points, but you always came back and pushed through. It wasn't easy, but you made it. You did something you had never done before. You're not anxious to turn around and hike the mountain a second time right away, but you Know you could if you needed to. After all, you've done it before. You could hike that mountain again or any other smaller mountain. You've already proven yourself.

Then your eye is drawn away in the wash of brilliant color painting the sky, and you suddenly find yourself staring at the distant peak of another, more distant mountain. A mountain you've never set foot on before. It's taller than the one you just crossed and the slopes look a little rougher. Still, you bet you could handle it. Deep down inside, a part of you almost hungers for the challenge—for the opportunity to stretch and prove yourself again. You just hammered out a towering peak; what's to stop you from taking on another one? Not today maybe, but soon. Very soon. You know you can hike up and over mountains now. You have Confidence that you can tackle them and survive. It'll be harder to take on a longer hike, to be sure, but you've already Experienced much of what a mountain might throw at you. You know what you need to bring and what you can leave behind. It doesn't hurt that the parking lot you're in now is higher than the one where you started. That gives you a head start on the next mountain. You just need to start moving your feet and stick to the path.

Debrief

Hopefully that story helps you to understand how the Belief Blueprint works from start to finish. You can see how the different stages aren't necessarily so tightly delineated. They kind of flow into each other. You can see how you start building Confidence with that first step you take. It starts out small and doesn't reach maturity until you complete your goal, but your positive Experiences immediately start building your Confidence and continue to do so until you reach the end destination and the culmination of your Confidence. At that point, your Confidence will boost you up and boost your Hope about new challenges and opportunities. The more mountains you climb, the stronger your belief will be that you can handle the next mountain you tackle.

Another point you can see is that your Hope never leaves you throughout the process. It is slowly "replaced" with Confidence in that thing, but it never leaves you because it just shifts targets. Once you've climbed the mountain, you can't simply Hope that you can climb it again. You've already done it. You *Know* you can do it again, but you can Hope that you can climb a different mountain and your Hope will be that much stronger because of the Experience and Confidence you gained by hiking this mountain.

Life is just like that. You tackle a goal, and you will know forever that you can do that thing again. The first time you tied your shoes on your own was a momentous day. From that time on, you've probably never wondered whether you could tie your shoe or not—at least you know you can tie them under normal conditions. Additionally, being able to tie your shoes gives you Hope that you can tie other things. You also have stronger Hope that you can learn different ways to tie things. Each new knot is a little easier to learn, and the whole process can become almost second nature. Additionally, each knot you learn helps you to be more Confident about the tying aspect of any situation where a knot is required. Learning to tie your shoes can help you feel more Hope about your ability to work a sail boat or go rock climbing.

Every mountain you hike up and over—every seesaw you tip—helps you to have that increased Belief that you can tip the next one too. Momentum, then, is a principle that works within a given goal and, more importantly, overall in your life. As you build Momentum within a goal, you'll be better able to achieve the goal. As you achieve your targets, you'll be building Momentum for your whole life, accelerating yourself and increasing your aggregate Belief. New tasks will seem less and less daunting because you'll be accustomed to tackling new things. The sum of your past victories will increase your understanding of how to Take Action and give you an increased desire to do so.

Triangular Feedback

When I first saw a basic model that became the basis of The Belief Blueprint, it had none of the tipping aspect that you've seen now. It actually looked very different than I've explained it, but it was still really helpful at the time and it changed my mindset. Back then, I was struggling in a new job. I'd been working at it for a while, but I didn't feel like I was breaking through. I certainly wasn't breaking through like I'd Hoped to. Things were progressing slowly, and it was getting really frustrating. I was starting to question whether or not I was even doing the right thing. You could say that my Doubts were growing more quickly than my positive Experiences.

That's when I had a mentor sit me down and show me the inspiration for the model I use today. When I originally learned about this model, I learned about it in a form more like this:

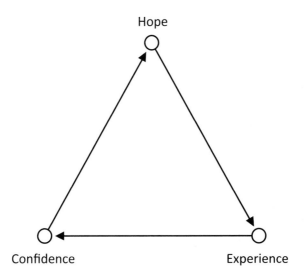

As you can see, it lacks some of the sophistication that I've discovered in it over the years. However, one thing it shows clearly is the relationship between Confidence and Hope. In the current model, it looks like you're done when you reach the Confidence end. And you *are* done when you reach the Confidence end...for that thing. Life isn't done yet though. Once you achieve the point of Confidence, you'll have successfully trained your limbic brain on that thing, and you will keep that training in your instincts forever. But that's only one aspect of your life, one target; the process doesn't stop there. The triangle diagram is really an over-simple representation of how we build our aggregate Belief. The Belief Blueprint is the model we follow to build every little Confidence that fills our bucket of aggregate Belief over time.

Once you climb one mountain, you'll be able to see the next peak more clearly. At that point, you will be able to leverage that newfound Confidence to boost your new Hope—the Hope you have of surmounting that next challenge. And the next and the next. Each time you accomplish a goal, you want to roll that Momentum straight into the next goal. Think of it as taking a running start. Whenever possible, don't sit around in between your goals. Be pleased with your results and progress, but don't be content with them. You want to stoke a fire inside yourself and strive to always be hungry. Always be pushing to take yourself to the next level.

That's the relationship shown in this older version of the model. Once you achieve Confidence in something, you'll have a better idea of how that thing works, opening the door to new levels of progress and achievement. Your Confidence will turn into Hope for a new possibility—the possibility of greater success and accomplishment. By using the model to create a pattern of progression for yourself, you can surely put yourself on a path to greatness. You can set yourself up to become the person you've always wanted to become—and then you can help others become their best selves too.

Reverse Gear

Unfortunately, I should explain that the model also works in reverse. Instead of leveraging Hope into Confidence and Confidence into Hope, some people choose (or don't choose) to go the opposite direction. For whatever reason, they focus on their negative Experiences and turn those against their Hope, eroding Hope into Despair. Then they use that Despair as a justification to attack everything and maybe everyone else in their lives until they are left with nothing except Despair. It's a sad situation, but it happens. Some people do it out of mental illness; others do it because they choose to—even if they don't "want" to. The truth is, it's a lot easier to let your Hope languish until it dies and turns into Despair. Maybe people choose this route simply because inactivity often appears to be the path of least resistance, at least initially.

If you're in this kind of vicious cycle, it's time to stop. It's never too late to turn things around, but you'll have to start small. The saying goes that "Hope springs eternal." That's true. The fading affect bias proves that the human brain is wired to Hope for good things, to favor good things. Sometimes the neocortex gets in the way and filters out the good. It's not easy to come back from that kind of paradigm, but you can do it. By focusing on good things, you can get your neocortex in line. In time, this will shift your confirmation bias away from all the negativity and toward the positive side of things. You might have to look hard at first, but it'll get easier to see those good things in time.

In fact, you can make that one of your first goals. You can Hope that you will feel Hopeful again and then Take Action to seek out uplifting elements in your life. You can search for Experiences that strengthen your Hope for the reality of Hope. Once you tip the Belief Blueprint, you'll be able to turn your sprouting Hope toward the next goal. You might need to start small, but you can turn the cycle around; just know that it's going to be hard at first. That's not a statement of discouragement. It's just a little realism so that you *don't* get discouraged. If you expect things to be impossible, you'll be pleasantly surprised when they're only difficult—so long as you have Hope and Belief that you can accomplish difficult things.

So give it time. If you've been locked into a cycle of negativity, it will take time to heal those wounds. The key will be to keep yourself under constant monitoring. Don't let yourself start to slip back into that negative cycle. Enlist mentors or accountability partners. Recruit your friends and family to help. Find new friends if you have to. As much as possible, either get the people around you to agree to be more positive or else put positive people around you. The company you choose to keep will have a big impact on your ability to stick with your change effort. After all, a recovering alcoholic won't be recovering very long if he chooses to hang out every evening at the bar with his old drinking buddies. You need to change your environment to whatever extent possible in order to reinforce your Hope for a better future.

Wrong Gear

Related to the idea of getting stuck in reverse is the idea of getting stuck in the wrong gear, or more accurately, going down the wrong path. Once you fully understand the Belief Blueprint and work to consciously implement it in your life, you'll need to be careful. This model is a way to become your very best self ever. You can build up Confidence after Confidence by achieving goal after goal to become better than you ever thought you could before. However, the model doesn't only work to build people up over time.

Unfortunately, the model can be used to whatever extent a person wants toward whatever end he or she wants. Most of us will use it to improve ourselves and the people around us. That's how we're wired. We want our lives to be better, and as we see the positive impact in our own lives, we want to reach out and help others to see the same results. Truly successful people (not necessarily rich people) want other people to have the same success. Among the truly successful, there's no scarcity mentality. Truly successful people believe there is more than enough success to go around for anyone who wants it. I hope that you feel that way.

However, not everyone leverages their selfish instincts into mutually beneficial actions and attitudes. There are people who would use this model to push their own agenda at the expense of others. The Belief Blueprint can actually equally explain how good people got better *and* how people like evil dictators rose to power. So check yourself and see which camp you belong in. Turning Hope into Confidence will work for anyone in anything, so just make sure that you're really going in the direction you want to before you set out. You don't want to head some distance down the path only to look back and realize that the mountain you wanted to climb is in the opposite direction. Choose your aim carefully.

Mountain Ranges

Now, going back to our analogy about the mountain hike, it probably seems a bit extreme to relate every goal to a snow-capped mountain. I agree. Not all goals are going to be equally taxing. Some are like Mount Everest (or even Olympus Mons, if you know what that is), and others are more like a pile of dirt in the backyard. Some goals can take a lifetime or more to fully achieve; others you could finish in a matter of days or even minutes. Goals come in all shapes and sizes, and they typically require preparation and focus in proportion to their level of difficulty. If you have a two-minute, molehill goal on your hands, you probably don't need to sit down and plan it out before you go. If you have an Everest goal on your hands, however, you might want to make yourself familiar with the major geography and set up a plan of attack. In life, you'll be hiking an entire range of mountains with a healthy scattering of hills, boulders, and mounds in between.

On a personal level, your mountains will all be different from each other. That makes sense because you don't really ever tackle the same goal twice, but the concept goes further than that. Not only are all your mountains different from one another, but your whole mountain range is different from everyone else's. Where learning to change your oil might be a towering, lofty peak for you, someone else might look at that as a single pebble. You agonize over it; he just steps over it—probably without even noticing. And this phenomenon isn't unique to auto repair; it holds true across every aspect of life. You may find it very easy to meet new people and form new friendships while a good friend of yours is extremely introverted. Each of us is different, so we each have different mountains in our ranges even if we have the same goals.

Lowering Your Fulcrum

This idea of different-sized mountains relates back to the Belief Blueprint because not all fulcrums are created equally in the same sense that not all mountains are created equally. Some fulcrums are much higher than others, just like with mountains. Let's take another look at the model and I'll help you see what I mean.

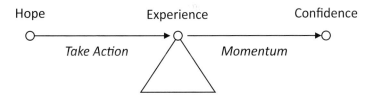

The fulcrum is that spot right in the center over which the rest of the model hinges. You can compare that fulcrum to the mountain. Bigger, more challenging goals and aspirations result in bigger, more challenging fulcrums. Smaller goals have smaller fulcrums. To help you see how this matters, imagine two different versions of the model, one with a low fulcrum and one with a high fulcrum.

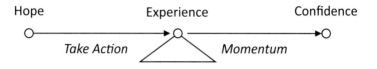

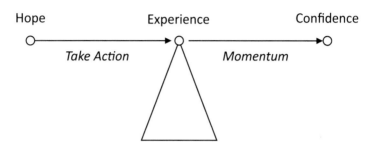

Now let's imagine that you sit on the one with the low fulcrum. How far are you going to fall? How steep is the climb from that initial position? It's not too bad, right? Now imagine sitting on the seesaw with the really high fulcrum. How far are you going to fall? Is the climb going to be a bit harder? The more complex or difficult a goal, the higher the fulcrum will reach, meaning that you'll have a steeper climb in order to reach that midpoint and tip the model into the Momentum side. Goals like this typically leave more failures in their wake if those attempting the goal don't understand this process of building Experience and Confidence.

The basic reason behind this is that the fulcrum, or height of the mountain, relates to your learning curve for that particular goal. The more you need to learn, the higher the climb you'll need to make. The problem people run into is that they take on a perfectly reasonable goal (like learning the piano) but don't think about the learning curve required. Because they don't take into account the complexity of the task, they end up disappointed when it takes more effort than they expected. This also plays in when you start on something new at the same time as someone else. Because of your different life Experiences and levels of related Confidence up to that point, your fulcrums for different goals will be different heights. What seems easy to you might be extremely difficult for your friend, or vice versa. So keep that in mind when someone else seems to be struggling with something you found to be easy. It's not necessarily a reflection on their commitment or intelligence or any of those things we normally blame. It could well be that they simply don't have the same preparatory Experience or natural aptitude that you do.

Which means you shouldn't be hard on yourself for struggling with something that seems to come easily to others, nor should you judge those who struggle while you excel. A lack of progress can't always be attributed to lack of ability. You and the individual you're observing simply don't have the same level of previous Experience. And that holds true even when you aren't comparing yourself to others because you are comparing yourself to your previous self instead. Remember, no two mountains are the same. No two fulcrums are the same height. You may have breezed right through a particular challenge, but that doesn't mean that you will breeze through all of them. On the flip side, getting hung up and struggling with a particularly high fulcrum doesn't mean that all your future fulcrums will be equally high. In fact, I'd say just the opposite is true. When you face a particularly high fulcrum and stick with it, you will gain just that much more Confidence on the back side. Think about it. When something is easy for you, does it boost you up as much? Large boosts to your Confidence come from conquering difficult challenges, not simple ones. You have to train harder and be in better shape to run a marathon than you do to run a 5k.

If you find yourself in a situation where you face a challenge you simply don't believe you're ready for, however, you still have options. You can go and face other challenges first. Every success you have— every Confidence you gain—will lower every other fulcrum in your life to some degree. Related Confidence and Experience can lower the fulcrum a lot. Unrelated things will only lower it a little. If you look up at that mountain and decide it's just too high to climb right now, climb the neighboring mountains instead and get to a higher starting place. It'll take longer, but it's a valid tactic. You don't generally come out of college and apply to be CEO of a Fortune 500 company, unless you're one of those overconfident types I spoke about previously. I'm not saying it couldn't happen, but you generally have to work your way up the ranks and gain Experience and Confidence for a while first. That doesn't mean you have to shy away from that daunting mountain, it just means you're going to do a few other mountains as warm ups before you come back and crush it.

Lengthening Your Arms

And doing other goals first isn't the only tactic for tackling those impossible high mountains. There is a workaround for taking on goals with higher fulcrums. The fulcrum represents (loosely) the amount of effort you have to put in in order to reach that turning point and push into the Momentum phase. The higher the fulcrum, the more effort you need to put in. This can be a bit overwhelming for people when they choose particularly difficult goals with high effort requirements. Thankfully, in addition to the height of the fulcrum, there's another variable we didn't really cover before when talking about the model in general terms. The steepness of the climb from Hope to Experience and over to Confidence depends heavily on the height of the fulcrum. However, there's another factor that can alter the level of effort required for forward progress. What about the length of the seesaw arms? Allow me to illustrate.

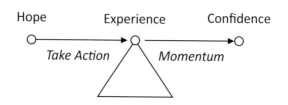

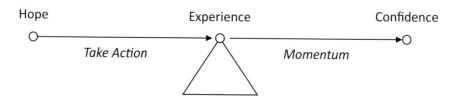

Imagine sitting on these two seesaws. Because the fulcrums are the same height, you'll actually fall the same distance regardless of the seesaw you climb on. So what's the difference? The difference is how steep the slope is from your new position at the start of the journey. With a short arm, you don't have to travel very far—but that means you need to cover a lot of vertical in very little time. The long arm means that it'll take a lot more time to cover that same vertical, but it means that you won't *feel* the amount of effort required quite as acutely. You have to put in the same amount of effort either way—that's determined by your relevant Experience and Confidence—but you don't necessarily have to put it in as quickly.

The length of the arms is related to the amount of time you have available for getting from Hope to Experience to Confidence. If you have all the time in the world, you can move slowly, which means that you won't have to cover so much vertical distance so quickly. This was like taking all the switchbacks in the mountain hike analogy I shared. If you were to hike straight up the mountainside, you could cover the same height in much less distance, but you'd be exerting your effort at a much higher rate. You're still trying to reach the same point, but by eliminating all the switchbacks, you'll reach it that much more quickly. On the other hand, you run a much greater risk of overextending yourself and burning out before you get to the peak.

So a smart move is to evaluate the difficulty of your goal and adjust your time horizon accordingly. If you want to take on a particularly difficult journey with a very high learning curve, you should probably budget more time for yourself to get the whole way through. This goes back to what I've said before about not expecting change overnight, but hopefully it helps you see why. If you can only put forward 5 units of effort each day and you need 100 units of effort to reach your goal, you can't take less than 20 days to reach the goal—and that assumes that you expend exactly no effort anywhere else.

Killer Comparisons

Where this really gets people down is when they start comparing themselves to others. They'll look at the 100 units of effort they need to reach the goal and compare it to the 80 units someone else needs. What people *don't* ever seem to look at is that the other person might have started at 200 units and just worked on it that much for that long. You never know where you started in relation to someone else, so it's never fair to yourself to make the comparison. Trying to pretend you have these kinds of answers is just a recipe for depression because people are so diverse that you'll always find someone out there who's better than you in a given thing. Then again, you'll be better than that person at something else, so it all sort of balances out. That's why it's a waste to compare yourself to others.

Additionally, it's a fact of life that some people just have more to give. This could be because of a natural ambition which drives that person to work longer, harder hours or it could just as easily be an absence of other obligations. If you have a family or friends, you're going to want to invest time into those relationships in order to strengthen and preserve them. With that in mind, the loner with no ties can almost always get more done than you because that loner doesn't have any other responsibilities. Would you really want to give up your family or friends in order to achieve your goals more quickly? Chances are that your family and friends play heavily into your goals, so leaving them wouldn't really make sense. That loner probably has a different set of goals and definitely has a different set of commitments than you, so stop comparing. Be fair to yourself and fair to that other person.

In the end, you need to realize that the journey up the mountain is always an individual one. You can (and should) talk to people who have gone before you and learn from their Experiences. You can (and should) enlist others to help you on your way. That being said, the ultimate effort always comes down to you and you alone. It's *your* Hope that will drive you, *your* Belief that will push you along, and *your* Confidence that will be gained in the end. No one can give you Confidence; you have to earn it for yourself. On the other hand, no one can take it away from you once you've earned it, so stop waiting for Confidence to magically appear in your life. Go out and find it. Set proper expectations for yourself and the commitment you're undertaking and then stick with it for as long as you need to in order to reach your goal. Don't quit just because it gets hard. Push forward with the strength of your Why and make yourself more than you were yesterday. Then make yourself more tomorrow than you are today. One day at a time, you'll become the person you've always wanted to be.

TAKE-AWAYS

And now you Know. You've seen and felt the power of the Belief Blueprint for yourself. You should be able to look back through your life and see plenty of times when this process worked for you—and probably some times when it worked against you. I hope that, by now, you've also started testing it. I hope you've started to apply it to your life, and I hope that it's bringing results, or at least perspective on how this works. In fact, my hope is that your life will be better as a result of learning the principles in this book. I hope that you're a better person today than you were yesterday and that you'll keep that tradition going tomorrow and the day after and forever. I want you to strive for perfection, but first I should probably tell you what that really means.

If you go back to the Latin from which the word "perfection" was taken, you learn that it doesn't actually mean flawless. That's a modern mistranslation, a modern adaptation for simplicity's sake. In reality, the Latin root means "finished" or "complete." Nowhere in that meaning is there any implication that there weren't mistakes made along the way. For better or worse, that view of perfection in modern western society comes from a Christian heritage and Jesus telling us all to be perfect like He is. Regardless of your belief in Jesus as the Son of God, let me point out something about this concept. Followers of Jesus believe that He knows we're all going to make mistakes along the way, so why would He give us a command that He knows we can't ever accomplish? Wouldn't that be a disaster? It's more of a translation issue as I've explained.

For me, He's not condemning me when He gives me that commandment. Instead, He's giving me the ultimate goal to always strive to be like Him—the highest mountain to climb. It's one I'll never reach the top of in this life, but that doesn't stop me from trying. According to the meaning of perfection, I can't reach that level until I'm complete anyway, and that can't happen while I'm still alive and gaining Experience. I won't be finished until I'm finished.

We've often heard the phrase, "you can't take it with you." This is referring of course to material possessions and worldly titles or accomplishments. But it's a core belief of mine that your eternal soul is tempered and shaped by the Confidences you attain in life, and therefore we do in fact take them with us into our next existence. Now if this isn't your belief, that's totally fine. Think of this process as shaping you for the rest of your life. I've just found that, for me, the idea of progression lasting forever has brought real perspective and meaning to the existence of mankind.

So, no matter who or what you believe or don't believe in, strive for wholeness. Work to make yourself the best you possibly can, and then work to make those around you better too. Together, you'll be able to work to bring each other up to a higher plane—making plenty of mistakes along the way. And that's okay. Learn from your mistakes and push forward again. When you fall, get back up. Focus on the positive side of things and make yourself the very best you can. With that in mind, I want to leave you with some key takeaways. Some of these things are punchlines that I've set up earlier, some are simply applications of the Belief Blueprint in ways that we haven't really covered yet. All of them are critical to your journey toward self-actualization and being your very best self.

The Tortoise and the Hare

First, I want to revisit a childhood memory. Remember when we talked about the Tortoise and the Hare? I brought it up to make the point that you need to just start moving. Your initial speed isn't as important as your focus on putting one foot in front of the other. Start Taking Action and keep Taking Action, and you'll get to your destination eventually. I was making that point to help you understand that you don't need to worry about sprinting; you just need to worry about getting started and then sticking with it. But there's more to the story than just going "slow and steady" to win the race.

There's something I didn't mention back then that I wanted to emphasize now. The Hare had far more ability—in terms of endurance and speed—than the Tortoise could ever dream of, yet the Hare "lost." Why? It's because of consistency. The Tortoise just stuck with it. That much you know. The Hare was all over the place in terms of engagement. Sometimes he was up at 100 percent, other times he was taking a nap or whatever else allowed the Tortoise a sporting chance. It would have been easy for the Hare to simply sprint to the finish line, but that wasn't the Hare's nature. The Hare was too flighty, too unfocused. Instead of staying consistent and steady, he wandered.

The Tortoise, on the other hand, was as steady as a rock. He plodded forward without tiring or getting distracted. The Tortoise didn't stop or detour or anything else. And here's the key: the Tortoise stayed 100 percent engaged the whole way. The Hare had bouts of engagement, but he didn't stay that way. The Tortoise couldn't move quickly, but he moved as quickly as he could. The problem I have with the story is the implication that "*slow* and steady wins the race." That's simply not true. Society has stewed that parable down to a sorry excuse for doing something halfway and getting away with it. The truth is that *steady* wins the race, slow or not. Slow was just an attribute of the Tortoise. Steady was his action plan. If the Tortoise could have moved more quickly, you can be certain that he would have. Winning that race meant everything to him, so he went all in. He didn't hold back and didn't get distracted.

That's how building Belief works. You put in consistent effort over time and you will build up the Experience that leads you to Confidence. A problem that I see so often is that people act like the Hare instead. They launch from the starting line at 100 percent and blast away (which is actually a great strategy if you can maintain it). For a time, they naturally make great progress, but they don't reach the finish line quickly enough, so they start to doubt themselves and throttle back. Then they have excess capacity, so they start to look for other ways to use that energy, other outlets, because they never earned the Confidence awaiting them after putting in steady effort over time. Pretty soon, they're working on something else and it is so cool and new that they divert even more attention and energy to it. Before long, they hardly remember the race they entered on that first goal. Instead, their focus is on the new thing, and when they look back, all they see is a failure. Frequently, they even manage to convince themselves that the venture was a dead end. That they never would have gotten anywhere even if they'd stayed with it. And that becomes their story. That's just a defense mechanism so that they don't have to face their own failure head on. It's much easier to blame other factors than your own lack of commitment and consistency.

People say that "If you always do what you've always done, you'll always get what you've always gotten." I don't think that's true all of the time. What if the Tortoise had listened to that kind of talk? The fact of the matter is that worthwhile endeavors always take time and go through periods of failure. As long as the goal is still valuable, you need to continue to pursue it with 100 percent focus—like the Tortoise. When you cease to be steady (at any speed), you open the door to distraction, discouragement, and despair. Sometimes, instead of needing to do anything different in order to get something different, you simply need to hold on a bit longer.

In Cub Scouts as a kid I remember doing a science experiment where we put cream and a little salt in a zipper bag and then smashed it around. For a long time, nothing seemed to be happening to the cream. It just sloshed around and around inside the bag. Then, after long minutes of what felt like nothing happening, the cream started to change. Then, within a very short time, it became butter. The thing is, that speedy conversion at the end would never have happened without the long, seemingly fruitless minutes of effort early on. If the kids lost patience and wandered off a few minutes in, we wouldn't have been around to see the change. So I say again, if your cause is worthwhile, stick with it. You never know when that cream is finally going to turn to butter.

The Right Moves

Of course, that raises a critical question. What would have happened to that poor Tortoise if he had set out on the wrong path at the beginning? His dogged persistence and steadiness would have only contributed to his own undoing. I get that. I'm not trying to say that you should never change gears or shift targets; I'm just saying that I see people lose focus and lose motivation far too often for far-too-trivial reasons. If you can step back and confirm that you're on the right path, why would you switch paths? Logically, that would only mean that you're switching from the right path to the wrong one. There are no shortcuts, remember?

So there's no reason to look around at everything else when you're pursuing a goal. That just opens you to distraction. If, however, you start to worry that you're not seeing the results you expected—you're not gaining the Experience you wanted—then it's a valid action to pause and make sure you're on course. Sometimes this means switching paths or switching vehicles, but don't default to looking for a change in vehicle. Every time you change vehicles, you will have to start over. You'll be able to carry in your Experience and Confidence, and that will lower the fulcrum height for you, but you'll still be starting small again. You'll be starting over with baby steps. You can't expect to change vehicles and maintain *all* the Momentum you've built up. You may keep your weight of Experience, but chances are that you'll lose some velocity as you aim your Hope at your new target.

The same principle holds true in leadership. Whenever you recruit someone to your team—either from within the organization or from outside—you are helping them change vehicles. As a result, they're going to be starting over to an extent. A common error is to recruit someone and then immediately ask that person to sprint forward with a task or assignment. Even if he or she understands the task and what's expected, there are always cultural implications to learn. You can think of this in terms of baby steps like we've discussed in the past. Whenever you recruit someone to a new position or new task, you are starting them on baby steps again. With that in mind, would you ask a toddler to run? If you did make that demand, what do you think would happen? The toddler would try but ultimately fall flat on the floor. Your new recruit is the same way.

So, when someone changes vehicles, don't immediately ask that person to run—even if that person is yourself. You need to give people time to get back up to speed. If he or she has plenty of relevant Experience and Confidence, it won't take long to get going again. If, however, he or she is learning something entirely new, there's going to be a learning curve. That fulcrum will need to be climbed before the new recruit is ready to blast forward. Be mindful of that. If you heap too much on a person too soon, you can overwhelm that person. Each new component adds an element of Doubt. Add too many components and that Doubt can overcome the person's Hope, pushing him or her into Despair. Your new recruit will burn out before they ever really got their feet under them. I think we can all agree that doing that to your people isn't leadership.

Instead, start people where their Hope and Experience is currently. Don't be afraid to stretch them, but work in small steps and build up to full speed. And remember to do that regardless of who the person is. So often, we are our own worst enemies. We might be patient and forgiving of others when they are trying something new but then not have those same qualities toward ourselves. Don't fall into that trap either. Be patient with yourself when you start out. It will take you a little time to get back up to speed just the same as anyone else. Give yourself that time. Push yourself, but don't overextend yourself. You'll be able to feel your own Doubts building up inside. When you feel that happening, take a moment and work on resolving some of them before you focus on moving forward again. You'll thank yourself later when you're enjoying the fruits of your labors.

Fundamental Attribution Error

Related to this concept is one that psychologists call the Fundamental Attribution Error. Basically, this error is an error in judgment. A simple example is that if you're at the grocery store behind someone and that person's credit card gets declined at the register, you naturally assume that he or she is overextended on his or her credit limit. Makes sense, right? What about when you step up and *your* card declines? You know you're not over your limit, so there must be some other reason. Perhaps your card has been shut down to protect you from possible fraud. Maybe the credit card terminal is broken. There's definitely another reason though. This line of thinking is what constitutes the fundamental attribution error.

This happens because we know ourselves and our circumstances, so we're inclined to give ourselves a fair shake when things happen. We attribute our successes to our hard, smart work, and we attribute our failures to environmental factors—often ones beyond our control. In a way, it's a defense mechanism to help us feel better about ourselves and how things are working out in our lives. When it comes to other people though, especially strangers, we tend to reverse the tables in a very unfair way. We often attribute the successes of strangers to their environmental factors (he was just in the right place at the right time) and attribute their failures to character deficiencies or conscious choices (he got pulled over because he was speeding because he's a bad, irresponsible person).

This error influences how we work with others in a potentially very negative way. When you assume that your coworker didn't finish her duties on time because she's lazy, you approach that conversation in a certain way. Your approach can largely color how the conversation plays out, and thanks to your confirmation bias, you'll only be seeing what reinforces your misguided Belief. This is another danger in leadership. If you approach problems and issues with your coworkers and teammates as being deficiencies in their ability or character, you will probably be overlooking very important warning signs and ruining chances to offer coaching and help.

Frequently, thanks to this error, we end up giving assignments to people which are beyond the person's current level of Experience. As a result, the person fails at the task and we attribute it to stupidity or laziness. In reality, most people don't go to work to be lazy. They go to work in order to work. Additionally, people are a lot smarter than we give them credit for. They might not know everything about all the same things as you, but they probably know a lot more about other things. You can see this sharply in the sci-fi geeks versus sports fans segments of the population. The sports fans can recite facts and statistics about their favorite teams, players, and sports. Sci-fi geeks can recite facts and statistics about Star Wars and Star Trek. Does that mean that either group is any less intelligent than the other group? I hope you answered "No." The problem is, we get into situations where we're working with people who have different interests and Experience. That person's level of Belief may be insufficient to accomplish the task, but that doesn't mean his or her ability is at fault. Even if the requisite skills are lacking, the deficiency might not actually be the missing ability. People can and will learn what they need to in order to perform—if given the chance.

So the next time someone on your team comes up short, consider whether it's a lack of training and support—experience—rather than a lack of desire or effort. Some people will beat their heads against the wall in a vain waste of effort rather than go to the boss and admit to not knowing how to do something. We're programmed to think that asking for help is a sign of weakness when it's really not. The ability to ask for help is a precursor to gaining great strength and knowledge. If you don't know how to do something, after all, how can you expect to learn if you don't ask someone to teach you? So you need to make sure that you're giving people the chance to learn by baby steps. You can't plunge people in over their heads because, try as they might, they won't be able to perform. Go ahead and put them in up to their necks and make sure they have access to the tools and training they need. That's the recipe for helping them perform.

Experience Thieves

Related to this is another instruction to the leaders out there. *Stop stealing Experiences from your people!* You may not know it, but you are probably stealing Experience from your people, thereby preventing them from gaining the Confidence they need in order to really perform for you. I know you're not doing it on purpose, but you might be doing it anyway, so let me explain how and what you can do to correct the behavior.

Let's say there's a conference coming up, and your team is in charge of preparing a segment for it. There are a couple of ways you can approach this scenario. First, you can just do it yourself. Second, you can delegate to your team and not worry about it anymore. Third, you can delegate to your team but then work with them through the process of preparation. What you decide to do will depend on the level of readiness in your team and your style of management, but it will also impact their future level of readiness.

Do It Yourself

The saying goes, "If you want something done right, you've got to do it yourself." There's certainly enough evidence for this concept in each of our lives. How many times have you asked someone else to do something—be it a child, coworker, boss, significant other, neighbor, friend, or whoever—and that person didn't come through? Even if he or she gave it a great effort, the vision was missed. The result fell short. And this happens sometimes even if you give clear, explicit instructions and set understandable expectations. People just see things differently and put a personal spin on it, departing from your original vision. As often as not, these alterations impact the final product in a negative way. After all, you understand how to do it, that's why you understood how to give the assignment. The only way around this problem is to do it yourself, right? It's okay to pass unimportant things over to the team, but the critical projects need to be done by you, right?

Not really. You don't really want to have to do everything—especially not everything important. You want to be able to share the load and duplicate your efforts. Well, you can't get to that point if you're always taking the lead on everything. This is the classic Experience thief situation. Each time you take over, sideline everyone else on the team, and try to run the complete play, you rob the rest of the team of the opportunity to perform and learn. You take away that chance for them to struggle and come off conqueror. You remove an opportunity to start with Hope, Take Action to build Experience, achieve Momentum, and gain Confidence.

I understand that most of us aren't doing this on purpose, but everything you do as a "favor" to your team to make life "easier" for them takes away a chance for them to learn how to cope with that challenge. I'm not saying that you should never do anything for your team, but if you want a capable team that can take initiative and make things happen, you need to give them chances to do just that.

Give It to the Team

So that leads to the second option: give it to the team. This must be the right choice, right? The team needs the Experience; your team members need the growth, right? So this must be the thing to do. Whenever a new project comes through, give it to the team and focus your efforts on tackling the routine assignments. That way you free up your team's time to be innovative and creative. You offload all the day-to-day tasks that they do without thinking anyway, and they are left fresh and ready for the big challenges. Sound like a perfect world?

Maybe. In many cases, teams will wear out under that kind of pressure over time, and will likely accuse the leadership of being lazy. They might initially relish the challenge, but it's hard to always be climbing and never really getting the chance to enjoy your Momentum. It's not that the work is any easier once Momentum is achieved, but it certainly goes more smoothly and more quickly. There's a sense of accomplishment that comes from cresting the mountain and tipping the Belief Blueprint, but that thrill is magnified by cruising down the downhill side to achieve the goal and the Confidence it entails. If you're only ever giving the new challenges to your people, they're always going to be scrambling up the model and never really getting the chance to see things through to the end. Not to mention that people get a huge boost of Confidence out of being able to step away from the challenges and do something they already know how to do—at least from time to time.

If people never get to go back and pound out something they're comfortable with, they run the risk of burning out. Robbing people of any challenges belittles them, but heaping only challenges on them is demotivating. It's tiring. It leaves people feeling like they can never get on top of what they're doing—it leaves them feeling Hopeless. It leaves them turning toward Despair. No matter how much Confidence they might build up from each successive challenge, at some point they'll break. They'll wonder why it never seems to get any easier. They'll question why they're even still around.

Work with the Team

Which brings us to the third option. This is the hybrid option and was kind of the obvious answer when I gave you the three choices earlier. In this option, you don't shield your people from challenges, but you don't leave them out there alone either. Your job as a leader—if you want to be a true leader—is to facilitate opportunities and Experiences in which people can build Belief, leading to Confidence. This is the best definition of leadership that I can think of. Your job is to facilitate Experiences that build Belief. This means that you let people do the things they are comfortable with, and then you push them to take on something new. If your child is comfortable riding a bike with the training wheels on, this is the part where you encourage that child to take off the training wheels. Then, taking it a step further, you don't just take off the training wheels and walk away; you stick around and help that child to learn balance and control. You hold the seat and keep him or her upright for a bit until they can balance the bike on their own.

When you get the assignment for that big presentation, you can do it yourself and rob your team of the Experience, you can give it to your team and leave them on their own, or you can give the assignment to the team and then work with them to learn how to build the presentation. This is the real purpose of having a team in the first place. As a leader, you need to mentor your people (or children, spouses, neighbors, friends, etc.) *and be mentored by them in return.* Everyone has a different skill set and a different set of Experiences. By working with the team, you can learn from their insights and build your own Confidence and Experience while helping them to do the same. You know you are leading correctly if you're learning from those you lead. It's a win-win situation.

And this goes for anything and nearly everything. You need to be thinking about who would benefit the most from an Experience regardless of how big or small that Experience will be. If it seems like a simple, easy task, you'll face a strong temptation to just knock it out and be done. What about that other person who could have benefited from gaining Confidence where you already have it? No matter how big or small the task is, your job as a leader is to identify what could be gained and then match that to the people who need to make those gains. Then you support those people through coaching and mentoring to help them make it through and gain the confidence.

To put into perspective just how often this can occur, let me tell you what happened just the other day. I was folding laundry and got to the socks at the bottom of the basket. My 4-year-old son was there watching me, and when he saw me fold the socks inside themselves, he was amazed. I've been folding socks for so long that I was way past the point of even noticing what I was doing, but my little boy was enthralled. So, trying to be a good parent, I asked him if he wanted a try. What ensued was almost painfully difficult for me.

I picked out a couple socks and gave them to him. Then I grabbed a couple for me and carefully, slowly, showed him exactly what he needed to do. He's a smart kid, but he's only four. Folding socks is a feat of dexterity at the limit of his ability. No matter how he tried, he couldn't seem to manage it. I can't express to you how hard it was to stop myself from just asking for the socks back and doing it myself. I'd have been done in two seconds or less. He was taking *minutes.* Still, it was a valuable opportunity for him to learn that I could be patient with him. It was also good for him to learn that he could screw up without the world ending. There were so many lessons for his little mind and heart to learn besides the technical aspect of folding socks, and I'd have crushed them all by taking those socks away.

When you work with people, don't take their socks. It might pain you to see them struggling to do something that seems so simple, but you can't intervene. If you do, you're only working to build dependency, not ability and Confidence. Even if it means more work for you, if your true motive is to help someone else improve, you have to let that person struggle. You have to let him or her work through the Blueprint. There are no shortcuts, and that includes "help" from another person. When you do something for someone, he or she won't learn. Keep that in mind and let your team struggle. Be there with comfort and counsel. Explain the Belief Blueprint to them so that they don't give in to Despair, but don't do it for them or you just rob them of the chance to grow. When an insecure member of my team asks me to help them with something I know they're capable of doing (or figuring out) for themselves, my response now is simply, "I can't take that Experience from you."

Summary

The Belief Blueprint works. It works for you or against you whether you're using it intentionally or not. It's the key to building Confidence over time, enabling you to do things in the future that would terrify you today. By following the model and putting it all together, you can improve your life and the lives of the people around you. The beauty of the model lies in its stunning simplicity. You have all the tools now to employ it in your life and then to mentor others to do the same.

In fact, I would ask that you go and do just that. I can only reach so many people myself. With this book, I hope to be able to touch many lives and help them to improve, to see where they are in their own Belief building, and to give them perspective and tools for getting to the next level. If you will go out and take this message to others, we can reach an exponentially higher number of people. We can improve lives everywhere for everyone in any circumstance. These principles aren't difficult to understand, in fact, now that you've read the book they seem painfully simple. But they typically remain undiscovered without a little outside assistance. Now that you've had that outside assistance, you can provide it to others. You can be a true leader—the kind that doesn't need title or power in order to lead. You can be the kind of leader that people look to for help because they know that you'll provide real opportunities for them to grow their Belief. That might feel intimidating right now, but keep tipping the seesaws of your goals toward Confidence and you'll be ready in no time. Just remember that the hallmark of the best leaders is service. True leaders look for ways to build others, to lift them. A leader who works for his or her own glory isn't really a leader at all. Be a true leader. It will enrich your life and enrich the lives of others. There is no greater reward than that.

CONCLUSION

After all is said and done, more is usually said than done. It's unfortunate but true. Don't let that be the case in your life. You know how the Belief Blueprint works. You know how to build Confidence in your life and build yourself up into the person you've always wanted to be. You actually already knew the path in your limbic brain, but now you know it in your neocortex too. Now you have the tools to get all the levels of your brain working together to put you on a path to meet and exceed your goals. You're on track to become what you've always wanted to become. Don't shy away from that.

It may be a daunting task to get started, but that's exactly what you need to do. We've talked about a lot of things, and I recommend you go back and look through them again. From time to time, skim through and remind yourself of what you learned. Teach the basics of it to someone close to you. You want to keep it fresh in your mind so that it can make the most impact in your life. Still, more important than all of that is your need to get out there and take the first step. It doesn't even really matter what your first step is. If you take the wrong one, you'll figure it out, backtrack, and take the first step again. You can repeat that process as many times as you need to in order to figure out where you're going. Remember, Hope will drive you and Hope paired with a worthy goal is velocity. Velocity is speed and direction. If you aren't moving, you can't really have speed *or* direction, so you can't have Hope.

Don't rob yourself of your most powerful asset by falling prey to what's often called "analysis paralysis." This is where you spend so much time trying to think through a task that you never get started on it. You're so busy gathering data and planning the attack that you never rally yourself and march. People do this all the time. Some do it out of an overzealous need to be efficient (ironically ruining their efficiency by never getting anything done). Others do it out of fear (there's no real danger in the planning stage). No matter what the temptation is for you, push through it. You'll get a clearer view as you move down the road, so start moving. Besides, as Helmuth Von Moltke famously said, "No operation extends with any certainty beyond the first encounter with the main body of the enemy." In other words, make your plans, but plan on contingencies because your original plan probably won't work out like you expect once you start moving. You'll realize that the variables have changed, you'll get a better view of what all the factors really are, and you'll alter all those painstakingly laid plans to better fit your new view of reality.

So, if I could leave you with just one lesson, it would be to start moving. Pick your goal and Take Action. If you'll do that, the rest will all come in time as you gain more Experience. That's the beauty of the Belief Blueprint. You don't even have to fully understand the model to make it work for you. Understanding the model just helps you to better focus and stick with the hard times in order to reach the success waiting on the other side. The critical lesson is to move your feet in the right direction. You'll refine your course as you move and get to your destination as long as you keep moving. I *Know* you can do it.

NOTES

NOTES